What Might Make Life Better?

Michael Welker | John Witte, Jr.

What Might Make Life Better?

On Character Formation, Ethical Education, and the Communication of Values in Late Modern Pluralistic Societies

WIPF & STOCK · Eugene, Oregon

Wipf and Stock Publishers
199 W 8th Ave, Suite 3
Eugene, OR 97401

What Might Make Life Better?
On Character Formation, Ethical Education, and the
Communication of Values in Late Modern Pluralistic Societies
By Welker, Michael and Witte, John, Jr.
Copyright © 2024 by Welker, Michael All rights reserved.
Softcover ISBN-13: 979-8-3852-4300-6
Hardcover ISBN-13: 979-8-3852-4301-3
Publication date 1/16/2025
Previously published by Evangelische Verlagsanstalt GmbH, 2024

This edition is a scanned facsimile of the original edition published in 2024.

Preface and Acknowledgments

This volume analyzes the powerful normative codes that, for better or worse, shape moral character and ethical education in late modern pluralistic societies. The chapters here build on and distill the findings of a six-year interdisciplinary study involving a hundred and fifty experts from Europe, North America, Australia, South Africa, and other liberal lands. We first analyze the shifting places and roles of these normative codes, both in the traditional social spheres of family, religion, law, politics, and markets, and in the comparatively newer social spheres of education, academic research, health care, the media, and the military. All ten of these social systems, we argue, remain essential for building a good life and a good society in late modern pluralistic societies today. But no social system, we submit, should be allowed to monopolize private and public morality and ethical education, and we suggest several pathways for these ten spheres separately and together to foster greater justice, freedom, benevolence, and peace at home and abroad.

We took on this ten-volume research project – and this concluding volume – to encourage readers to move beyond vague popular talk about late modern pluralistic societies and to map more clearly how these societies are structured and how they influence the moral character formation and ethical value systems of their members. "Late modernity" today is a capacious term used to describe the social conditions of Western liberal lands over the past few decades. In this late modern era, the unique individual person, rather than the community or its associations, is viewed as the center of agency and responsibility. The term "pluralism" for many today thus means a multicolored "plurality" of human individuals, together with a few long-standing groups and associations, such as the family, church, or business, that are voluntarily formed and dissolved – each offering generous rights of entrance and exit for individuals. Liberal-minded people have welcomed this late modern plurality as a source and structure of freedom and creative development opportunities. Conservative-minded people – and, of course, numerous opponents of all forms of pluralism, historically and today – still see plurality as a breeding ground for social and ethical instability, for fostering and featuring an ethic of "anything goes" so long as no harm is done.

Our project challenges this conventional understanding of pluralism as mere plurality – whether from a liberal or a conservative perspective. We demonstrate instead that late modern societies are characterized by what some call "multisystemic pluralism" or what we call "structured pluralism." By this, we mean that, in reality, modern liberal societies comprise a variety of social systems or social spheres, which interact with each other and with individuals in complex ways. While any of these spheres or their combinations can become dangerous and damaging, they are nonetheless essential for their preservation and flourishing of complex liberal societies, and they play critical roles in the character formation and ethical education of each new generation of individual members. We believe that understanding structured pluralism as a complex division of powers and value systems provides more nuance than Jürgen Habermas's earlier worries about "the new complexity" of modernity, or Armin Nassehi's more recent lament about "the overburdened society."

This is the latest in a twenty-five-year series of interdisciplinary projects on which the two of us have happily collaborated – on such topics as human nature; human rights; religion and globalization; religion and science; the concept of law in religion, science, and legal studies; the interaction of law and religion; and the Protestant Reformation's impact on church, state, and society. We bring different but overlapping disciplinary interests and methods to this collaboration. Michael Welker is an interdisciplinary theologian with expertise in Christology, the doctrine of the Holy Spirit, creation theory, anthropology, eschatology, religion and science, and biblical theology. John Witte is an interdisciplinary jurist with expertise in legal history, human rights, religious freedom, marriage and family law, and law and religion.

We have sought to combine our efforts in writing this volume. We have each written five chapters – some at the core of our expertise, some more peripheral. Michael took the lead in writing the chapters on the forms and norms of character formation and ethical education offered by the spheres of religion, education, academic research, health care, and the media as well as in writing the concluding reflections. His chapters focus on the main findings of the individual experts whom we gathered for each interdisciplinary research group. John took the lead in writing the chapters on the family, law, politics, the market, and the military as well as in writing the introduction. His chapters are more historically grounded and provide comparative overviews of the topic of each research group, with the chapters of individual experts referenced more fully in the footnotes. We hope that these twin approaches to our topic in this capstone volume give readers a vivid sense of what is on offer in these ten volumes and encourage them to take up individual chapters and themes in those volumes.

We have incurred several debts in creating and co-leading this six-year project and completing this capstone volume. We are deeply grateful for the hundred and fifty international scholars who participated in one or more of the ten roundtable conferences hosted principally by the Research Center for International and Interdisciplinary Theology (Forschungszentrum Internationale und Interdisziplinäre Theologie – the FIIT) at the University of Heidelberg, directed by Michael Welker. These conferences proved to be invaluable interdisciplinary explorations that helped define and refine the methodology of our project as a whole and to illustrate how each of the ten social spheres has shaped public and private morality in older liberal societies in Europe and North America, and in the more recently established liberal democracies of Australia, South Africa, South Korea, and elsewhere. Several University of Heidelberg and FIIT colleagues provided vital support for these roundtables. The student assistants Christine Böckmann, Viola von Boehn, Hans Joachim Kenkel, David Reissmann and Daniel Stil helped us greatly in the organizing of the consultations, the administration of the finances, and the preparation of the books for publication. Several consultations happened at the FIIT and at the International Academic Forum of the Heidelberg University (IWH). All these efforts were further supported by the faculty and staff of the Center for the Study of Law and Religion at Emory University, directed by John Witte, and the faculty and staff of the Public and Contextual Theology Research Centre at Charles Sturt University, Australia, directed by Bishop Stephen Pickard.

We are deeply grateful for the sponsorship of several generous benefactors: the Karl Schlecht Foundation (which, together with the University of Heidelberg, supported the conference and volumes on the market and the family); to the Public and Contextual Theology Research Center, Charles Sturt University, Canberra (for support of the publication of the volume on the military); and above all the McDonald Agape Foundation (which sponsored the conferences and volumes on academic research, education, health care, law, media, religion, and political economy). Furthermore, the McDonald Agape Foundation – and its president and chairman, Peter McDonald – have also generously supported the preparation of this capstone volume and the convening of an international public conference at the University of Heidelberg in December 2024, featuring a score of contributors to the ten volumes.

This ambitious project would not have been possible without the invaluable collaboration and expert counsel of several distinguished scholarly friends: Professor Dr. Juergen von Hagen (Bonn), Professor Dr. Piet Naudé (Stellenbosch), Bishop and Professor Dr. Stephen Pickard (Canberra), and Professor Dr. William Schweiker (Chicago). These four scholarly giants not only helped to lead the ten individual roundtables but also lent their expertise in coediting and contributing chapters to several of the volumes. In addition, at a time when COVID prevented international travel and in-person roundtables, Professor Dr. Eva Winkler (Heidelberg) kindly stepped in to co-lead the consultation and follow-up volume on health care, and Bishop Stephen Pickard did the same for the consultation and volume on the military.

We are deeply grateful to Dr. Gary S. Hauk – historian emeritus of Emory University, former chief of staff to four Emory presidents, and most recently senior editorial consultant in the Center for the Study of Law and Religion – for his exquisite work in editing and copyediting each of the ten volumes in this series, together with this capstone volume. Gary has a remarkable ability to edit scholarship from a variety of disciplines written by scholars from different cultures and linguistic traditions, and we benefited greatly from that skill. We give further thanks to Layla Maie Koch for translating several chapters for the final volume into German, and to the editors at Evangelische Verlagsanstalt in Leipzig and at Wipf & Stock in Eugene, Oregon, for taking on these volumes and marketing them in Europe and North America.

Michael Welker, Universität Heidelberg
John Witte, Jr., Emory University

Table of Contents

Introduction	13
Chapter 1	17
The Marital Family	17
The Family in Society: Historical Patterns and Modern Trends	18
The Modern Family and Character Formation	23
Concluding Reflections	31
Chapter 2	33
Religion and the Church	33
Religion as a Differentiated Sphere in Late Modern Societies	35
Critical Perspectives on the Project	39
Justice, Mercy, and Faith in Pluralist Context	42
Chapter 3	45
Politics and the State	45
Political Forms and Moral Formation	45
Modern Politics in Interdisciplinary Perspective	47
Chapter 4	53
Law and Justice	53
Chapter 5	65
Health Care	65
Costs versus Care	66
Hard Ethical Decisions and Trade-offs in Health Care	69
The Challenges of Nursing	71
Health Care in Interdisciplinary Perspective	72
Concluding Reflections	73
Chapter 6	75
Academic Research	75
Ethics and Research Universities	75
Character and Ethics at the Intersection of Disciplines	80
Conclusions	85

Chapter 7 ... 87
Education and Schools ... 87
Religious and Psychological Resources for Education ... 88
Education and Character Development in Comparative Perspective ... 91
Old and New Challenges in Education ... 93

Chapter 8 ... 95
The Market and Economics ... 95
Markets Are Essential Institutions ... 95
Do Markets Encourage Moral Character Formation? ... 97
Are Markets Amoral? ... 99
Do Markets Harm Moral Character Formation? ... 101
Concluding Reflections ... 104

Chapter 9 ... 107
Media and Communication ... 107

Chapter 10 ... 115
The Military and Character Formation ... 115
Character Formation and Soldierly Virtues ... 117
The *Miles Protector* ... 117
Innere Führung ... 118
The Reciprocal Influence of Military Virtues and Societal Values ... 119
The Price of Serving: The Effects of Military Service and Challenges of Reintegration ... 120
Psychological and Moral Injuries ... 121
Reintegration Challenges for Veterans and their Families ... 121
Public Perception ... 122
Acknowledgment and Support ... 123
The Role of the Church in Military Ethics and Peacebuilding ... 124
Spiritual Care ... 125
Christian Advocacy ... 125
Concluding Reflections ... 126

Concluding Reflections: Enduring Issues, New Challenges ... 129
The Family ... 130
Religion ... 131
Politics ... 133
Law ... 134
Health Care ... 135

Academic Research	137
Education	139
The Market	140
Media	141
The Military	143

Introduction

Five hundred years ago, Protestant reformer Martin Luther argued that "three estates" (*drei Stände*) lie at the foundation of a just and orderly society: marital families, religious communities, and political authorities. Parents in the home, pastors in the church, princes in the state: these, said Luther, are the three authorities whom God appointed to represent divine justice and mercy in the world, to protect peace and liberty in earthly life. Household, church, and state: these are the three institutional pillars on which to build social systems of education, charity, and economics. Family, faith, and freedom: these are the three things that people will die for.

In the half millennium since Luther, historians have uncovered various classical and Christian antecedents to these early Protestant views. And numerous later theorists have propounded all manner of variations and applications of this three-estates theory, many increasingly abstracted from Luther's overtly Christian worldview. Early modern covenant theologians, both Christian and Jewish, described the marital, confessional, and political covenants that God calls human beings to form, each directed to interrelated personal and public ends. Social-contract theorists differentiated the three contracts that humans enter as they move from the state of nature to an organized society protective of their natural rights: the marital contract of husband and wife; the government contract of rulers and citizens; and, for some, the religious contracts of preachers and parishioners. Early anthropologists posited three stages of development of civilization: from family-based tribes and clans, to priest-run theocracies, to fully organized states that embraced all three institutions. Sociologists distinguished three main forms of authority in an organized community: "traditional" authority that begins in the home, "charismatic" authority that is exemplified in the church, and "legal" authority that is rooted in the state. Legal historians outlined three stages of development of legal norms: from the habits and rules of the family, to the customs and canons of religion, to the statutes and codes of the state.

Already a century ago, however, scholars in different fields began to flatten out this hierarchical theory of social institutions and to emphasize the foundational role of other social institutions alongside the family, church, and state in shaping private and public life and character. Sociologists like Max Weber and Talcott Parsons emphasized the shaping powers of "technical rationality" exemplified especially in new industry, scientific education, and market economies. Legal scholars like Otto von Gierke and F. W. Maitland emphasized the critical roles of nonstate legal associations (*Genossenschaften*) in maintaining a just social, political, and legal order historically and today. Catholic subsidiarity theories of Pope Leo XIII and the social teachings movement emphasized the essential task of mediating social units between the individual and the state to cater the full range of needs, interests, rights, and duties of individuals. Protestant theories of sphere sovereignty, inspired by Abraham Kuyper and neo-Calvinists, argued that not only churches, states, and families but also the social spheres of art, labor, education, economics, agriculture, recreation, and more should enjoy a level of independence from others, especially an overreaching church or state. Various theories of social or structural pluralism, civil society, voluntary associations, the independent sector, multiculturalism, multinormativity, and other such labels have now come to the fore in the ensuing decades – both liberal and conservative, religious and secular, and featuring all manner of methods and logics.

Pluralism of all sorts is now a commonplace of late modern societies. At minimum, the concept has come to mean a multitude of free and equal individuals and a multitude of groups and institutions, each with very different political, moral, religious, and professional interests and orientations. It includes the sundry associations, interest groups, parties, lobbies, and social movements that often rapidly flourish and fade around a common cause, especially when aided by modern technology and social media. Some see in this texture of plurality an enormous potential for colorful and creative development and a robust expression of human and cultural freedom. Others see a chaotic individualism and radical relativism, which endangers normative education, moral character formation, and effective cultivation of enduring values or virtues that cater to a common good.

Pluralism viewed as vague plurality, however, focuses on only one aspect of late modern societies – the equality of individuals, and their almost unlimited freedom to participate and associate peaceably at any time as a respected voice in the moral reasoning and civil interactions of a society. But this view does not adequately recognize that, beneath this shifting cacophony of social forms and norms that constitute modernity, pluralistic societies have heavy normative codes that shape their individual and collective values and morals, preferences and prejudices.

The sources of much of this normative coding and moral education in late modern pluralistic societies are the deep and powerful social systems that are the pillars of every advanced culture. The most powerful and pervasive of these are the social systems of family, religion, politics, law, economics, education, academic research, media, health care, and the military. The actual empirical forms of each of these powerful social systems can and do vary greatly, even in the relatively homogeneous societies of the late modern West. But these deeper social systems in one form or another are structurally essential and often normatively decisive in individual and communal lives today.

Every advanced society has family systems of love and procreation, religious systems of ritual and doctrine, political systems of authority and liberty, legal systems of justice and order, economic systems of trade and property, media systems of communication and dissemination of news and information, and educational systems of preservation, application, and creation of knowledge and scientific advance. Many advanced societies also have massive systems of science, technology, health care, and military power with vast influence over and through all of the other social systems. These pervasive social systems lie at the foundation of modern advanced societies, and they anchor the vast pluralities of associations and social interactions that might happen to exist at any given time.

Each of these social systems has internal value systems, institutionalized rationalities, and normative customs and expectations that together help to shape each individual's morality and character. Each of these social spheres, moreover, has its own professionals and experts who shape and implement its internal structures and processes. The normative network created by these social spheres is often harder to grasp today, since late modern pluralistic societies usually do not bring these different value systems to light under the dominance of just one organization, institution, and power. And this normative network has also become more shifting and fragile, especially since traditional social systems like religion and the family have eroded in their durability and power, and other social systems like science, health care, the market, military, and media have become more powerful.

The aim of this volume is to identify the realities and potentials of these core social systems to provide moral orientation and character formation in our day. What do, can, and should these social spheres, separately and together, do in shaping the moral character of late modern individuals who, by nature, culture, and constitutional norms, are free and equal in dignity and rights? What are and should be the core educational functions and moral responsibilities of each of these social spheres? How can we better understand and better influence the complex interactions among individualism, the normative binding powers of these social systems, and the creativity of civil groups and institutions? How can we map and measure the different hierarchies of values that govern each of these social systems, and that are also interwoven and interconnected in various ways in shaping late modern understandings of the common good? How do we negotiate the boundaries and conflicts between and among these social systems when one encroaches on the other, or imposes its values and rationalities on individuals at the cost of the other social spheres or of the common good? What and where are the intrinsic strengths of each social sphere that should be made more overt in character formation, public education, and the shaping of minds and mentalities?

These are some of the guiding questions at work in a ten-volume project that we have led, involving some hundred and fifty scholars across the academy – scholars from the humanities, social sciences, and natural sciences as well as the professions of theology, law, business, medicine, and more. This project has drawn on case studies from Western Europe, North America, South Africa, and Australia, which together provide just enough diversity to test out broader theories of character formation, ethical education, and the communication of values. While most of our scholars come from the Protestant and Catholic worlds, our endeavor is to offer comparative insights that will help scholars from any profession or confession. While our laboratory is principally Western pluralistic liberal societies, the modern forces of globalization will soon make these issues of moral character formation a concern for every culture and region of the world – given the power of global social media, entertainment, and sports; the pervasiveness of global finance, business, trade, and law; and the perennial global worries over food, health care, environmental degradation, terrorism, warfare, and natural disasters.

This volume builds on and distills the main findings and broader themes to emerge from our interdisciplinary study. We first analyze the shifting places and roles of these normative codes and their interactions in the social spheres of family, religion, law, politics, markets, education, academic research, health care, the media, and the military. We then map out several pathways for these ten spheres separately and together to foster greater justice, freedom, benevolence, and peace, and to make life better for persons and peoples at home and abroad.

Chapter 1

The Marital Family

The family is humanity's oldest and most basic social institution.[1] It has long been regarded as the cornerstone of social organization and character formation. Aristotle and the Roman Stoics called the marital family the "foundation of the polis" and "the private font of public virtue." The Church Fathers and medieval Catholics called it the "seedbed" of the city, "the sacramental force that welds Christian society together." Protestants and Enlightenment philosophers alike called the family a "little church", a "little commonwealth", the "seminary of the republic", the "first school" of love and justice, nurture and education, charity and citizenship, discipline and production.[2] Echoing these traditional insights, modern evolutionary scientists now argue that humans developed enduring pair-bonding family structures of reproduction and nurture as the fittest means for long-term survival and success as a species.[3] Modern social scientists

---

[1] This chapter distills the findings and arguments set out in: John Witte, Jr., Michael Welker, and Stephen Pickard, eds., *The Impact of the Family on Character Formation, Ethical Education, and the Communication of Values in Late Modern Pluralistic Societies* (Leipzig: Evangelische Verlagsanstalt, 2022) [hereafter *Family and Character*]. See also John Witte, Jr., *Church, State, and Family: Reconciling Traditional Teachings and Modern Liberties* (Cambridge: Cambridge University Press, 2019); and Stephen M. Tipton and John Witte, Jr., *Family Transformed: Religion, Values, and Family Life in Interdisciplinary Perspective* (Washington, DC: Georgetown University Press, 2005).

[2] See detailed sources in John Witte, Jr., *From Sacrament to Contract: Marriage, Religion, and Law in the Western Tradition,* 2nd ed. (Louisville, KY: Westminster John Knox Press, 2012).

[3] See, for example, Bernard Chapais, *Primeval Kinship: How Pair-Bonding Gave Birth to Human Society* (Cambridge, MA: Harvard University Press, 2008); Melvin A. Konner, *The Evolution of Childhood: Relations, Emotions, Mind* (Cambridge, MA: Harvard Uni-

have shown that the stable marital family is a critical source of happiness and flourishing for most adults and children, and a vital embodiment and teacher of the moral norms and habits needed to navigate the worlds of religion, law, politics, economics, education, communication, health care, and more.[4] The Western tradition has long taught that while the marital family is neither good for everyone nor always good, it offers essential private goods to most couples and children and vital public goods to society.

The Family in Society: Historical Patterns and Modern Trends

Historically in the West, the term "family" covered a range of domestic relationships. The nuclear family – comprising husband and wife and their natural, adopted, or stepchildren – was long at the heart of the Western family. But until modern times, the family household also often included one or more grandparents, siblings, aunts, uncles, and other blood relatives. Sometimes it also included live-in servants, apprentices, and students – slaves sadly, too, in some Western countries, until the abolition of slavery in the nineteenth century.[5] Classically, the household was under the authority of the *paterfamilias* – the husband, father, and master, or, in his absence, the *materfamilias* or a close male relative. While the heads of the family had ample autonomy, they were guided by family law codes, household manuals, confessional books, and catechetical texts that set out the religious, moral, and civic duties and rights of husband and wife, parents and children, masters and servants, and the family's obligations to church, state, and society.[6] When families were broken by death, desertion, or divorce, family relatives played critical roles in as-

---

versity Press, 2010); and Frans B. M. de Waal, *A Tree of Origin: What Primate Behavior Can Tell Us about Human Evolution* (Cambridge, MA: Harvard University Press, 2002).

[4] See, for example, Don S. Browning, *Marriage and Modernization: How Globalization Threatens Marriage and What to Do about It* (Grand Rapids: Eerdmans, 2003); and detailed annual reports by the National Marriage Project at the University of Virginia http://nationalmarriageproject.org/ and the Institute for American Values, http://www.americanvalues.org/.

[5] See, for example, Steven E. Ozment, *Ancestors: The Loving Family in Old Europe* (Cambridge, MA: Harvard University Press, 2001); and John Witte, Jr. and Gary S. Hauk, eds., *Christianity and Family Law: An Introduction* (Cambridge: Cambridge University Press, 2017).

[6] See, for example, James A. Brundage, *Law, Sex, and Christian Society in Medieval Europe* (Chicago: University of Chicago Press, 1987); and Steven E. Ozment, *When Fathers Ruled: Family Life in Reformation Europe* (Cambridge, MA: Harvard University Press, 1983).

suming care of dependent children, needy adults, and elderly kin who were left.[7] While remarriage was theologically discouraged – and forbidden in Catholic lands for divorced persons – it was often essential for surviving, let alone thriving, in earlier societies, particularly given prohibitions on nonmarital cohabitation.[8] Until well into the twentieth century, and in many places still today, widows, divorced persons, orphans, and nonmarital children fared far worse than those in stable and loving marital families.[9] And the problems of these unattached parties deepened in times of war, drought, flood, epidemic, or other disasters, or when these parties faced systemic gender, religious, or racial discrimination.[10]

Historically, and in some quarters still today, the family embodied and imparted essential norms, habits, and values for living in other social institutions. The family was a vital *religious* unit in society – a site of daily prayer and devotion, of catechesis and spiritual formation, of ritual observance and piety, and of pastoral care and comfort, and sometimes the venue for formal house churches.[11] The family was a vital *legal* unit – the most immediate and pervasive locus of authority and liberty, of rights and duties, of rules and judgments, of punishment and reward, of mercy and equity. The family was a vital *economic* unit – especially historical households with attendant fields, shops, services,

---

[7] See examples in Michael J. Broyde, "'Hearts Will Never Be Practical until They Can Be Made Unbreakable': What Does Parental Love Really Mean in Hard Cases in the Jewish Tradition?", in *Family and Character*, 179–97; and Andreas Kruse, "Old Age within the Polyphony of Sensations, Experiences, and Commitments in Favor of the Neighbor", in *Family and Character*, 163–78.

[8] On the complex theology of remarriage, see John Witte, Jr., *The Western Case for Monogamy over Polygamy* (Cambridge: Cambridge University Press, 2015).

[9] See detailed sources and discussion in John Witte, Jr., *The Sins of the Fathers: The Law and Theology of Illegitimacy Reconsidered* (Cambridge: Cambridge University Press, 2009).

[10] See, for example, Enola Aird, "Toward a Renaissance for the African American Family: Confronting the Lie of Black Inferiority", in *Family and Character*, 233–46; Katja Patzel-Mattern and Sabina Pauen, "Family Structures and Values in Postwar Germany", in *Family and Character*, 291–312; and Nadia Marais, "'A Most Sacred Covenant': John Calvin's Rhetoric of Marriage and Its Implications for Transmitting Values in South Africa", in *Family and Character*, 312–32.

[11] See, for example, Marcia Bunge, "Communicating Values by Honoring Families and the Full Humanity of Children: Lessons from Robust Theologies and Detrimental Developments Among Protestants", in *Family and Character*, 105–26; and Richard R. Osmer and Katherine M. Douglass, eds., *Cultivating Teen Faith: Insights from the Confirmation Project* (Grand Rapids: Eerdmans, 2018).

and servants which depended on and contributed to stable markets.¹² The family was a vital *educational* unit that not only provided children with their first instruction in reading, writing, and arithmetic but also provided apprenticeships and vocational training central to personal success in economic, political, and religious life.¹³ The family was a vital *welfare* institution that provided essential security and provision for parents, children, and other kin, for caring and sharing, nutrition and nursing, poor relief and elder care.¹⁴ And the family was a distinct *property* unit – whose formation often occasioned property exchanges between two families, and whose dissolution opened a new channel for transmitting property to remaining household members and other heirs.

Not only did the family anticipate and prepare its members for participation in other social institutions, but the family also was deeply interwoven with other social institutions and dependent on them for support and service.¹⁵ Churches and states have long played key roles. The church was, and for some today still is, an essential site for marital preparation and weddings, for baptism, catechesis, initiation, and confirmation, for family worship and communal celebration. The church often provided elementary education for children, pastoral care for parents, diaconal support for needy families, and sometimes mediation and dispute resolution for troubled or broken families. And the church was the usual site of funerals and for the intense support systems needed by grieving family members.

Before the sixteenth-century Reformation, the church also governed marriage and family life through its canon laws and church courts. After the Reformation – in Protestant lands and eventually in Catholic lands, too – the state set most of the basic rules and procedures for marital formation and dissolution, for spousal care and support, for parental rights and duties, for public education and vocational training, and for preserving, distributing, and transmitting family property across generations. State officials also intervened in severe family disputes, crises, or dysfunction, and, when necessary, helped to dissolve marital families, divide family properties, and reassign parental responsibilities. With the rise of the modern welfare state over the past century, state regulations

---

[12] See Jürgen von Hagen, Michael Welker, and John Witte, Jr., eds., *The Impact of the Economy on Character Formation, Ethical Education, and the Communication of Values in Late Modern Pluralistic Societies* (Leipzig: Evangelische Verlagsanstalt, 2020) and further chapter 8 herein.

[13] Stephen L. Carter, "Religion, Education, and the Primacy of the Family", in *Family and Character*, 247–54; and Margaret F. Brinig, *Family Law and Community: Supporting the Covenant* (Chicago: University of Chicago Press, 2010).

[14] Patrick Parkinson, "The Role of Public Policy in Supporting Safe, Stable, and Nurturing Families in Late Modern Societies", in *Family and Character*, 211–22.

[15] The next two paragraphs are distilled from Witte, *Church, State, and Family*, 197–202.

and bureaucrats have sought to regulate and aid the family much more closely than in the past. This has triggered the rise of countervailing constitutional privacy and domestic autonomy claims that have ebbed and flowed in strength in modern courts.

Other associations have also long played key roles in support of the family. Legal professionals registered the marriage certificates and marital properties of the newly married couple. They helped enforce, amend, and dissolve the contracts of marriage and marital property. They summoned the legal resources to support and protect wives and children from neglect and abuse, and, when necessary, arranged for adoptions, guardianship, and other forms of institutional care and protection. Lawyers litigated marital and family disputes in state courts and sometimes church tribunals. They helped probate the wills and administer the trusts that are vital to the transmission of the family name, business, and property to the next generation. Medical professionals, in turn, taught new family members the basics of nutrition and hygiene, fitness and aging, childcare and development. They provided support and care to families during pregnancy and childbirth, sickness or bereavement, abuse or divorce. Medical professionals helped ease a person's pain and burdens in the final steps of life, and they certified death, with all the emotional, spiritual, and legal consequences that follow from this final declaration.

As modern Western societies have become more differentiated and specialized, other associations and their professionals have become critical for marriage and the family as well, sometimes crowding out traditional support systems. Therapists now provide much of the psychological and practical counseling for courting couples, broken families, and grieving divorced or widowed persons. Accountants now participate in a good deal of a family's economics – filing taxes, planning school funds, and devising trusts, wills, and estates. Day care centers provide a good deal of childcare for working parents. Schools and universities now organize a great deal of the formal education and vocational training. Clubs and associations – scout troops, athletic teams, and neighborhood groups – now provide children with socialization and skill development. Modern marketers and media – particularly with the rise of the internet – now furnish family members with direct access to all manner of information, commodities, and experiences. Hospitals and clinics, nurseries and hospices now deliver much of the family's health care from the beginning of life to the end.

Such was – and in some quarters still is – the family ideal for many citizens. But by no means for all. For our ancestors, the family could be a site of tyranny and abuse, of poverty and deprivation, of cruelty and loneliness, of wastrel and wanton living from which there was little escape or recourse. Wife abuse, exploitation, and deprivation have caused and continue to inflict massive and lasting harm on women. This domestic abuse continues today, albeit slowed by strong new movements of women's rights, stern new measures of criminal law, and striking new #MeToo and other self-help movements. Likewise, fetal abuse by alcohol or drugs together with physical, emotional, and verbal child abuse, neglect, deprivation, undereducation, inadequate health care, rape, sexual exploitation, and other afflictions mangle and scar a child's body, mind, character, and spirit for life. This devastating harm to children has continued at an alarming rate in modern liberal societies, let alone the rest of the world, despite strong new children's rights provisions, escalating punishments for felony child abuse, and the exponential rise of child welfare agencies, both public and private.[16]

Moreover, the marital family altogether as an institution has become much more fragmented and fragile in late modern liberal societies.[17] In the past half century, many countries have shrunk the formal and functional differences between marital life and nonmarital cohabitation, and they have removed many of the traditional supports reserved for marital families. Strong new privacy laws protect all manner of voluntary sexual interactions among consenting adults, and rapidly growing portions of the population are "drifting into sex and parenthood without marriage."[18] To be sure, some 90 percent of college-educated and relatively well-to-do citizens now form stable marital families and rear their children in intact homes – markedly stronger numbers than thirty or forty years ago at the height of the sexual revolution, with its 50 percent divorce rate.[19] The authorization of same-sex marriage in recent years has strengthened the numbers of stable marital families.[20] But in North America, for those with fewer means and less education, "marriage rates are low, divorce rates are high, and a first child is more likely to be born to parents who are single than to parents who

---

[16] Jean Bethke Elshtain, "The Heart of the Matter: The Family as the Site of Fundamental Ethical Struggle", in *Family and Character*, 197–210; and Helen M. Alvaré, *Putting Children's Interests First in US Family Law and Policy: With Power Comes Responsibility* (Cambridge: Cambridge University Press, 2017).

[17] Browning, *Marriage and Modernization*; and Gordon S. Mikoski, "'The Times They are A-Changin'': Shifting Patterns of Partnering and Parenting in the United States and Implications for Religious Transmission and Theology", in *Family and Character*, 233–32.

[18] Isabel V. Sawhill, *Generation Unbound: Drifting into Sex and Parenthood without Marriage* (Washington, DC: Brookings Institution Press, 2014).

[19] See detailed annual statistics and analysis by the National Marriage Project at the University of Virginia, http://nationalmarriageproject.org/ and the Institute for American Values, http://www.americanvalues.org/.

[20] Patrick Hornbeck, "Religious Liberty and Family Diversity: The Legal and Theological Disputes", in *Family and Character*, 255–74; and Jonathan Rauch and David Blankenhorn, "Marriage Opportunity: The Moment for National Action", http://americanvalues.org/catalog/pdfs/Marriage-Opportunity.pdf.

are married."[21] And compared to children born and raised in intact loving marital families, these nonmarital children usually have less than half the educational and vocational success, and nearly triple the rates of school dropout, tobacco, drug, and alcohol abuse, teenage pregnancy, truancy, delinquency, criminality, and eventual incarceration.[22] The rates of nonmarital cohabitation and procreation are higher in most parts of Western Europe, Latin America, and Australasia today, even while many of these modern liberal nations are losing the cultural cohesion, political consensus, and economic capital needed to maintain the modern welfare state that, for the past century, had absorbed many of the responsibilities historically discharged by the church and family.[23]

The Modern Family and Character Formation

It is easy to lament the breakdown of the modern Western family and the seeming slide into a sexual state of nature where life is "nasty, brutish, and short" – particularly for women and children, as well as for the poor, sick, elderly,[24] and disabled bereft of reliable kin altruism, diaconal care, or social welfare. But happily, in recent years, leading scholars, advocates, policy makers, and religious, cultural, political, and public-health officials in liberal lands have responded decisively in leading a powerful new promarriage and profamily movement. This movement combines traditional teachings and modern social science and public-health findings to advocate for stable marital families, responsible sex and parentage, and proper family planning as essential for private flourishing and social stability.[25] And this movement has pressed for robust new church,

---

[21] June Carbone and Naomi Cahn, *Marriage Matters: How Inequality Is Remaking the American Family* (Oxford: Oxford University Press, 2014), 19–20; see also Melissa Kearney, *The Two-Parent Privilege: How the Decline in Marriage Has Increased Inequality and Lowered Social Mobility, and What We Can Do* (London: Swift Press, 2023).

[22] Ibid.; Alvaré, *Putting Children First*; and Margaret F. Brinig and Steven L. Nock. "Can Law Shape the Development of Unconditional Love in Children?", in *The Best Love of the Child: Being Loved and Being Taught to Love as the First Human Right*, ed. Timothy P. Jackson (Grand Rapids: Eerdmans, 2011), 317–46; id., "'I Only Want Trust': Norms and Autonomy", *Journal of Socio-Economics* 32 (2003): 471–87.

[23] Browning, *Marriage and Modernization*; and Witte, *Church, State, and Family*, 300–35.

[24] Ibid.; Andreas Kruse, "Old Age within the Polyphony of Sensations, Experiences, and Commitments in Favor of the Neighbor", in *Family and Character*, 163–78; and Emil K. Abel, *Elder Care in Crisis: How the Social Safety Net Fails Families* (New York: NYU Press, 2022).

[25] Don S. Browning et al., *From Culture Wars to Common Ground: Religion and the Family Debate*, 2nd ed. (Louisville, KY: Westminster John Knox Press, 2000); Robert P. George

state, and economic policies in support of the stable marital family[26] – including, notably, stable same-sex families in most Western countries today.

Part of this profamily movement requires us to rethink the place and role of the marital family in late modern liberal societies and the interaction of the family with other powerful social systems. Perhaps the modern family is no longer the "foundation of the polis", as Aristotle wrote, or "the cornerstone of Western civilization", as the United States Supreme Court confidently pronounced.[27] Perhaps the modern family can no longer operate as the "little church", the "little commonwealth", and the "little school" and "seminary of the republic" as fully as it once did, given the emergence of so many powerful new forms of social organization with their shaping influences on public and private morality. But the stable marital family, we submit, remains an essential institution in late modern liberal societies that still embodies and imparts norms, values, skills, and experiences that are essential for navigating and flourishing in the network of modern social institutions. Several recent studies have borne this out.

First, social scientists have documented at length the critical role of family mechanisms and experiences that guide social learning and moral formation in early childhood. The family is a "mini-cosmos" for a young child, leading German scholars Sabina Pauen and Katja Patzel-Martin write, and what a child experiences in those first few years shapes their entire being, value system, and moral capacity for life. Infant children need, above all, a safe, stable, and loving environment so they can bond with loving parents, siblings, and other caretakers. These bonds not only satisfy an infant's physical needs, but more importantly meet their innate human need to trust other humans – the "nucleus of social relatedness." In a loving family, infants learn early how to distinguish and practice prosocial and antisocial behavior, to witness and experience empathy and shared emotions. Toddlers already learn cooperation, sharing, spontaneous helping, limits, and rewards, as well as the first steps of navigating conflicts of interest with their siblings and peers. By the age of five or six, most children start to develop a "true sense of morality" and understand the true differences between right and wrong, and the reasons for the rewards and reprimands that follow. They learn "self-regulation skills" and the capacity to take an "external perspective" on their own behavior. Only then can they begin to develop feel-

---

and Jean Bethke Elshtain, eds., *The Meaning of Marriage: Family, State, Markets, and Morals* (Dallas, TX: Spence Publishing Co., 2006); and John Witte, Jr., *In Defense of the Marital Family* (Leiden: Brill, 2023).

[26] Parkinson, "The Role of Public Policy"; id., *Family Law and the Indissolubility of Parenthood* (Cambridge: Cambridge University Press, 2011); and Daniel Cere and Linda M. McClain, *What Is Parenthood? Contemporary Debates about the Family* (New York: NYU Press, 2013).

[27] Aristotle, *Politics*, 1.1.1; and *Reynolds v. U.S.*, 98 U.S. 145, 164–66 (1879).

ings of shame and pride, and the ability to discern, discuss, and deploy basic social values and elementary morality.²⁸

> If caregivers respond consistently, consequently, and appropriately to prosocial and antisocial behaviors of other family members, young children will find it easy to develop basic trust, impulse control, and a positive self-concept. If parents talk with their children about emotions and mental states frequently, this will support children's development of empathy and theory-of-mind competencies. And if caregivers are also good role models, this promotes the process of internalizing values and norms.²⁹

Love begets love", echoes American family ethicist, Stephen G. Post. And a loving and faithful family typically produces children – whether natural-born or adopted – who are more likely than not to be caring, compassionate, conscientious, and "morally creative."³⁰ "The apple does not fall far from the tree", is a homey saying to underscore that children often emulate their parents and families; good characters tend to beget good characters most of the time.

Second, in the family, both adults and children learn the arts and values of communication, ritual, and narrative. Communication is "the dynamic side" of community, Anglican theologian Oliver O'Donovan writes, the essential means and method of building "common interest", and a sense of the common good.³¹ As social creatures, we inhabit many communities of communication – political communities into which we are born, religious communities into which we are initiated, neighborhood communities in which we live, and sundry other communities that we inhabit or seek out for work, play, education, investment, pleasure, consumption, art, science, health care, services, and more. Each of these communities has its distinct norms and forms of communication that convey meaning, purpose, promise, or friendship.

But the most sublime, intense, and enduring forms of communication usually occur within the marital family.³² In a healthy marriage, spouses are the

---

[28] Sabina Pauen, "The Beginnings of Norm and Value Formation in Human Ontogeny and the Role of the Family", in *Family and Character*, 59–73; see also Patzel-Mattern and Pauen, "Family Structures and Values in Postwar German Society"; and Sabina Pauen, *Vom Baby zum Kleinkind: Entwicklungstagebuch zur Beobachtung und Begleitung in den ersten Lebensjahren* (Heidelberg: Spektrum Akademischer Verlag, 2011).

[29] Pauen, "The Beginnings of Norm and Value Formation", 72.

[30] Stephen G. Post, "Love Begets Love and It Starts in the Family", in *Family and Character*, 127–38.

[31] Oliver O'Donovan, *Entering into Rest: Ethics as Theology*, vol. 3 (Grand Rapids: Eerdmans, 2017), 47–48.

[32] Ibid., 63–64, 140–46.

most intimate: they communicate their deepest feelings, passions, fears, aspirations, intuitions, and experiences with each other. In marriage, spouses are the most vulnerable: they share their very life, body, memories, health, happiness, well-being, food, money, and material goods with each other. And in marriage, spouses are the most fully committed: marriage carries an expectation of fidelity, loyalty, and permanence that is communicated in the daily sharing of life, home, bed, and board and goes beyond that of any other community.

Communication is also at the heart of the relationship of parents and children from infancy to adulthood. Parents communicate their very substance to their children – their genes, we now say, coded and coated with their instincts, inclinations, talents, strengths, weaknesses, resiliencies, and vulnerabilities. Mothers communicate their very bodies, blood, and being with their children throughout pregnancy, and then provide their newborns with life-giving food and drink through nursing. Parents share the tender singing, cooing, rocking, cuddling, and caressing that communicate the deep feelings of love and tenderness so vital to a child's well-being and healthy development. Developmental psychologist Erik Erikson once wrote that the first "greeting ceremonial" between a mother and a child "is the root of all subsequent ritualization" and communication.[33]

Ongoing robust verbal and symbolic communications within the family are vital for each child's healthy emotional, social, and moral development. This symphony of family communications occurs in morning and bedtime rituals, long table talks and family storytelling during meals, trips, walks, and other routine experiences of daily life. It occurs when reading, playing, praying, working, and interacting with parents, siblings, friends, and kinfolk, and when maturing children witness the loving communications of their parents and grandparents and other family members.[34] It occurs as siblings and relatives slowly spin and stitch together the fabric of symbiotic attachment that can last a lifetime, and that siblings can often pick up easily again, even after long intervals of silence and separation. Leading family psychologist Robyn Fivush has shown how important these intrafamily rituals, narratives, and storytelling are for routinizing and grounding the lives of children and preparing them for the intense and diverse forms and forums of communication at work in other social institutions. Particularly shared family stories, Fivush shows, "create, sustain, and nurture strong emotional connections between family members." They "provide

---

[33] Erik Erikson, "The Development of Ritualization", in Donald R. Cutler, ed. *The Religious Situation* (Boston: Beacon Press, 1968), 711–33, quoted and discussed in Robert N. Bellah, "Marriage in the Matrix of Habit and History", in Tipton and Witte, *Family Transformed*, 21–33, at 25.

[34] See, for example, Robyn Fivush and Judith A. Hudson, eds., *Knowing and Remembering in Young Children* (Cambridge: Cambridge University Press, 2013).

an anchor that allows children and adolescents to explore who they are with the safe knowledge that they have a strong foundation." And they "display family values and morals" and provide "models of forgiveness, of sharing and love, of everyday moral decision-making, of rectifying injustices and standing up for others and oneself."[35]

To be sure, radio, television, and especially the internet now bombard children and families with all manner of communications about commodities, experiences, values, needs, relationships, and alternative models and modes of morality – and immorality, with the wildest frontiers of pathos now only a mouse click away. Parents and other family members have shrinking control over this pervasive new form and forum of communication, especially for their online adolescent and teenage children. Parents and caretakers, in turn, are themselves often distracted by these pervasive media, or use them as substitutes for their own communication and childcare – from parking toddlers in front of the television for hours on end to mollifying moping adolescents with cell phones and iPads that attract heavy use.[36]

Child development psychologists have raised the alarm on how corrosive and dangerous it is for children to be raised unsupervised and unguided in this pervasive modern information age. They have warned parents and teachers about the slick and seductive social media that build both addictions and attention deficit disorders in children. Young and adolescent children need protection not only from the disturbing media depictions of pornography, violence, hatred, and more. They also need protection from the marketers and media designers who work skillfully and steadily to cultivate all manner of interests and perceived needs in their audiences, specifically targeting children at each stage of their development. Family specialists are rapidly developing a whole industry of parental guides for their and their children's responsible and productive use of the media that is more consistent with the essential forms of personal intrafamilial communication and ethical education. And educational and media companies, in turn, are working to develop constructive and edifying websites, shows, and programs for the healthy nurture and education of children at various stages of their development.[37]

---

[35] Robyn Fivush, "Family Storytelling and the Communication of Values", in *Family and Character*, 90–109, at 90, 108–09.

[36] Bunge, "Communicating Values"; Elshtain, "The Heart of the Matter"; see further Michael Welker et al., eds., *The Impact of the Media on Character Formation, Ethical Education, and the Communication of Values in Late Modern Pluralistic Societies* (Leipzig: Evangelische Verlagsanstalt, 2022), and further chapter 9 herein.

[37] Eric N. Holmes, *Children and the Internet: Legal Considerations in Restricting Access to Content* (Washington, DC: Congressional Research Service, 2022); Adam Butler, *Monsters in the Closet: Exposing Real Threats to Children and Teenagers in the Home* (Eugene,

Third, in a stable loving family, young children develop not only basic social values, moral capacities, and communications skills. They also learn to appreciate and articulate basic legal concepts of right and wrong, authority and liberty, promises and expectations, mine and thine. American jurist Harold J. Berman put this well in describing how young children first give voice to the moral "law written on their hearts."[38]

> Children intuitively sense this law within us. Every child in the world will say, "That's my toy." That's property law. Every child will say, "But you promised me." That's contract law. Every child will say, "It's not my fault. He hit me first." That's tort law. Every child will say, "No, I didn't; ask him." That's evidence law. Every child will say, too, "Daddy said I could." That's constitutional law. Law ultimately comes from our human nature, and our human nature is ultimately an image of God, the source of all law.[39]

Historically, and in some religious households still today, parents and caretakers work hard to cultivate and elaborate these inborn legal and moral intuitions by teaching children about the moral laws of God. The Hebrew Bible encouraged daily instruction in the many detailed rules of the Mosaic law: "You shall teach them diligently to your children, and shall talk of them when you sit in your house and when you walk by the way, and when you lie down and when you rise."[40] "Train up a child in the way he should go, and when he is old he will not depart from it."[41] These and other biblical passages, and their many parallels in childhood literature and household manuals over the centuries,[42] have inspired a long and deep tradition of reflection about how critical teaching and learning the laws of God, church, state, and family are for grounding a child's basic ethical orientation and appreciation for the moral duties owed to God, neighbor, and self.

OR: Resource Publications, 2020); Barrie Gunter, *Children and Television Consumption in the Digital Era: Use, Impact, and Regulation* (London: Routledge, 2021); and Thomas J. Shaw, *Children and the Internet: A Global Guide for Lawyers and Parents* (Chicago: American Bar Association, 2012).

[38] Romans 2:15.
[39] Quoted and discussed in John Witte, Jr., *Faith, Freedom, and Family: New Studies in Law and Religion*, ed. Norman Doe and Gary S. Hauk (Tübingen: Mohr Siebeck, 2021), 219.
[40] Deuteronomy 6:6–9.
[41] Proverbs 22:6.
[42] See, for example, Judith Evans Grubbs et al., eds., *The Oxford Handbook of Childhood and Education in the Classical World* (Oxford: Oxford University Press, 2014); and Nicholas Orme, *Medieval Children* (New Haven: Yale University Press, 2001).

Children need to learn not just the rules – the "condensed codes" of legal and moral conduct as British anthropologist Mary Douglas called them: "do this" and "don't do that."[43] They also need to learn what Douglas called the "elaborated codes": the explanations for why the rules are constructed the way they are, what purposes they serve, and how to apply them in solving individual cases and dilemmas. By this, children gain an essential elementary understanding of law, equity, and justice – the law on the books and the law in action. From *Aesop's Fables* to *Winnie the Pooh,* from *Sesame Street* to *Mr. Rogers' Neighborhood*, children's books, shows, and other media are filled with stories of delicious moral conundrums and legal dilemmas that help a young child learn how to reason through what is better or worse, fairer or harder for the characters they encounter. Through their parents and teachers, adolescent and teenage children are taught to think through the increasingly complex moral and legal problems of social living and to read literature, watch films, and perform in debates and dramas that slowly broaden their canon of knowledge and capacity for casuistry. Children are not "empty vessels", writes child development expert Eugene Roehlkepartain. They come not only with inborn legal and moral instincts and appetites. They also have their own "humanity, agency, and dignity" which makes them "dynamic partners" in the cultivation of their legal and moral capacities and behavior.[44]

Fourth, in the family, children also learn, by observation and experiment, basic economic concepts, values, and practices. Pastoral theologian Bonnie Miller-McLemore has shown that through daily household chores, children learn the value of labor and its importance for the common good of the household. Through weekly allowance and savings accounts, and trips to the store or shopping online with their parents, they learn the elementary skills of buying and selling, of investing and accumulating. Through volunteer work in their neighborhoods, clubs, churches, and other communities, they learn the elementary responsibilities and routines of loving their neighbor. Through their schoolwork, they gain the knowledge, skills, and capacities to discern their vocation in life and the discipline needed to excel and flourish at whatever they feel called to do.[45] Lutheran ethicist Marcia Bunge has shown how important this

---

[43] Mary Douglas, *Natural Symbols: Explorations in Cosmology* (London: Barrie and Jenkins, 1973), 24–26, discussed in Bellah, "Marriage in the Matrix of Habit and History", 23–27.

[44] Eugene C. Roehlkepartain, "Empty Vessels or Active Agents? Amplifying Young People's Agency in Character Development in their Families", in *Family and Character*, 147–62. See also John Wall, *Ethics in the Light of Childhood* (Washington, DC: Georgetown University Press, 2010).

[45] Bonnie J. Miller-McLemore, "Children, Chores, and Character Formation: A Child-Centered Perspective", in *Family and Character,* 89–104.

cultivation of a sense of vocation is to affirm the "creativity, humanity, and agency" of children:

> Regardless of country or worldview, if families and the network of institutions that surround and support them – particularly faith communities, schools, and the state – consistently honor and emphasize the full humanity of children, we can unleash many creative energies in families and communities for supporting child well-being and passing on values that help societies and individuals of all ages thrive and flourish.[46]

To be sure, some historical and modern families and communities mercilessly exploit children and their labor. Historically, families had many children to supply the back-breaking manual labor in the fields and family shops, which could be deeply corrosive to a child's well-being and healthy development. With the centuries-long trans-Atlantic slave trade, black children were reduced to chattel commodities to be bought and sold at the whim of their masters, often separated from their parents and siblings, and toiling without relief, protection, or compensation throughout their oft-short lives. With the modern Industrial Revolution, children, especially from poorer or broken families, were sent into the factories, mines, and building sites, with ample risk to their lives and limbs and sometimes tragic exploitation by adult supervisors and fellow workers. With the rise of the modern military complex and the escalation of devastating modern wars, young adults have been pressed or conscripted into dangerous military service. With the modern global sexual revolution, millions of children in both developing and liberal countries have been tragically pimped and sold into sexual trafficking, servitude, and slavery.[47]

Mercifully, both modern liberal governments and international children's rights agencies have worked hard to outlaw abusive child labor and exploitation of all sorts, and to mandate and pay for children's education, social welfare, and health care until young adulthood. Mercifully, modern labor and workplace regulations have made work outside the home safer, healthier, and less exploitative in liberal lands for adults and youth alike. And mercifully, modern economists have come to regard work both within and beyond the home as equally valuable to individuals and societies. And in this restructured and reimagined family environment, the judicious use and loving cultivation of economic and labor skills

---

[46] Bunge, "Communicating Values", 124–25. See further Marcia J. Bunge, ed., *The Child in Christian Thought* (Grand Rapids: Eerdmans, 2001); and Marcia J. Bunge, ed., *Children, Adults, and Shared Responsibilities* (Cambridge: Cambridge University Press, 2012).

[47] See sources and discussion in Miller-McLemore, "Children, Chores, and Character Formation", and in Witte, *Church, State, and Family*, 238–73.

and experiences for children has proved critical to their growing capacities as adults.[48]

Finally, in modern liberal societies, the stable marital family home remains for many a "haven in a heartless world", in Christopher Lasch's apt phrase.[49] Ideally, the family home is a unique place of permanent safety and security, of familiarity and comfort, of regularity and predictability, of privacy and protection. Ideally, the family home is a permanent sanctuary for children at any stage of their lives, no matter how "prodigal" they may have become, no matter how far down the sultry "highways" of life they may have run, or the "byways" of life they may have crawled.[50] Ideally, the family home is a place where all family members can expect love and nurture, comfort and encouragement, direction and discipline, forgiveness and forbearance. Ideally, the family home is the one place in the world where a person can be him or herself, can be completely open, authentic, and vulnerable. Whether returning from a day's work or school or from a long trip or semester away, whether arriving in glory or shame, triumph or need, children and adults alike instinctually know that "there's no place like home."

Concluding Reflections

The modern family is thus a distinct social institution of love, care, and hope and an institution deeply interwoven with other social institutions. Modern schooling, work, leisure, consumption, worship, legal regulation, and public administration all shape and color the ways we court and marry, bear and raise children, make and break family bonds. At the same time, most people see marriage and family life at the heart of what makes life worth living and essential to a society worth living in and working for. Marriage and family life not only realize romance but also inspire hard work and justify key aims of public policy and provision. In this sense, it does take a society, with all of its diverse institutions, to raise a family. And the breakdown of families causes severe private and public harms that rapidly ripple throughout a community.[51]

To be sure, many modern scholars "do not really much like the idea of institutions", leading sociologist Robert Bellah has noted. Critics argue that institutions like marital families are holdovers from the past, built on "largely unex-

---

[48] Ibid.
[49] Christopher Lasch, *Haven in a Heartless World: The Family Besieged* (New York: Basic Books, 1979).
[50] Luke 15:11–32 (parable of the prodigal son).
[51] This paragraph is adapted from Tipton and Witte, introduction to *Family Transformed*, 1–2.

amined traditions and habits" and resistant to our current needs and desires. "Institutions are oppressive, at the extreme one thinks of prisons and mental asylums, and they limit our free individual choice."[52] Some scholars today thus call for the "deinstitutionalization", "disestablishment", or "abolition" of the marital family.[53] "Marriage is a great institution, if you like living in institutions", Paula Ettelbrick put it memorably.[54]

Such criticisms are helpful reminders that all social institutions, including the marital family, must remain coherent, contained, and conducive to private and public goods, and always open to reform and improvement both in their forms and functions.[55] But it is dangerous to abandon or abolish the institution of the marital family and to leave matters of sex, reproduction, and childcare entirely to unfettered and unstructured free choice. After all, it was the very dangers and violence of a sexual state of nature that forced men and women to form organized societies, with their distinct marital, political, religious, and other voluntary institutions. Brilliant thought experiments about deinstitutionalization and disestablishment of the family are easy enough to draw up on the blackboard or on a blank page or screen. But they are much harder to do in real time and cultural space, with the realities of ongoing social life and the momentum of time-tested customs and family practices. As Bellah put it: "Although every imaginable criticism of institutions, including the institutions of marriage and the family, has some basis, without institutions we would not be free, we would be dead. In every aspect of our lives we depend on the relationships that institutions make possible."[56] And the family institution remains, for many, the first institution to nurture, support, and shape our character and morality.

---

[52] Bellah, "Marriage in the Matrix of Habit and History", 21. See further Robert N. Bellah et al., *The Good Society* (New York: Vintage Books, 1991), 287–306.

[53] Witte, *Church, State, and Family*, 336–78.

[54] Paula L. Ettelbrick, "Since When Is Marriage a Path to Liberation?" *Outlook: National Gay and Lesbian Quarterly* 6 (Fall, 1989): 9, 14, quoted and discussed in Stephen Macedo, *Just Married: Same-Sex Couples, Monogamy & the Future of Marriage* (Princeton: Princeton University Press, 2015), 80–85.

[55] Parkinson, "The Role of Public Policy."

[56] Bellah, "Marriage in the Matrix", 21–22.

Chapter 2

Religion and the Church

"Religions are in inexorable decline worldwide!" In 1968, the *New York Times* published this prediction by renowned American sociologist Peter Berger. According to Berger, religious believers in the twenty-first century would "probably be found only in small sects that flock together to resist a worldwide secular culture."[57] Thirty years later, Berger had to admit that his prediction had been proven wrong. He now declared the world to be "post-secular", and many took his word for it.[58] Various international statistics on people's religious affiliation bear this out: "In 1970, the percentage of people worldwide who professed some form of religion was 80.8 percent. By 2000, however, this percentage had risen to 87.0 percent, and it continues to grow."[59] Since 2000, many parts of the world today have in fact witnessed a new "great awakening" of religion – a resurgence of traditional religions and the rapid growth of a wide variety of new or newly prominent forms of faith.

Not so much in late modern Western liberal lands, however. In marked contrast to these global patterns of religious resilience and resurgence in the new

---

[57] Peter Berger, "A Bleak Outlook Is Seen for Religion", *New York Times*, Feb. 25, 1968.
[58] Peter Berger, "The Desecularization of the World: A Global Overview", in *The Desecularization of the World: Resurgent Religion and World Politics*, ed. Peter Berger (Grand Rapids: Eerdmans, 1999), 1–18. Particularly resonant: Jürgen Habermas, *Glaube und Wissen. Friedenspreis des Deutschen Buchhandels* (Frankfurt: Suhrkamp, 2001); Jürgen Habermas, *Auch eine Geschichte der Philosophie*, 2 vols. (Frankfurt: Suhrkamp, 2019); and Franz Gruber and Markus Knapp, eds., *Wissen und Glauben: Theologische Reaktionen auf das Werk von Jürgen Habermas 'Auch eine Geschichte der Philosophie'* (Freiburg: Herder, 2021).
[59] G. A. Zurlo, T. M. Johnson, and P. F. Crossing, "World Christianity and Religions 2022: A Complicated Relationship", *International Bulletin of Mission Research* 46, no. 1 (2022): 71–80 (Michael Welker translation), https://doi.org/10.1177/23969393211046993.

millennium, modern Western liberal societies have seen a dwindling of traditional religious resonance and charisma over the past half century. Especially in economically and scientifically influential liberal countries in North America, Europe, and Australia, many Christian churches and other religions have been steadily losing members and thus influence since the 1960 s. Until the nineteenth century, Christian churches led Western societies in teaching and modeling norms and habits of morality and character. This was done through the churches' services and sacraments, their creeds and catechisms, their schools and charities, their monasteries and health-care facilities – all of which were designed to habituate and demonstrate the cardinal commandments to love God, neighbor, and self. Today, by contrast, many critics claim that churches and other organized religions are outdated, abusive, dangerous, and discriminatory. Religious freedom, once taken for granted as a cornerstone of the Western constitutional order, is now very much up for grabs in many liberal societies, especially when religious freedom clashes with strong new demands for sexual freedom, self-determination, and personal autonomy.

As a consequence, Christianity and other religions have taken a subordinate institutional and intellectual role in many Western lands. Markets, media, medicine, military, and massive scientific education and economic enterprises have taken over much of the moral leadership, shaping both public customs and culture as well as private morality and ethics. Moreover, many businesses, academies, and political institutions have distanced themselves from traditional religious institutions and ideas, and often now base their work on purportedly nonreligious foundations and logics. In many families and schools, too, churches have lost considerable weight and influence in the daily lives of their members. Even within the sphere of organized religions, major surges in valuing privatization and individualization have called into question and eroded traditional church forms, content, and authority – a trend exacerbated by COVID isolation and the new habits of worshiping from home, if at all.

Religion has not died, however, in Western liberal democracies. The United States Supreme Court in the past decade has strengthened religious freedom protections, enabling churches and other faith traditions to become more popular, publicly influential, and politically active again (albeit disproportionately on the political right). In Europe, even while many traditional established churches remain mostly empty on Sunday mornings, new forms and forums of faith are on the rise, aided by the porous boundaries and powerful migration movements born of the European Union and Council of Europe. Similar patterns can be seen in Australia, South Africa, and other liberal democracies. Moreover, both traditional and new forms of religiosity in Western liberal lands have found new ways to navigate our modern technological cultures – skillfully using both markets and social media to teach their faith, to reach their faithful, to offer their educational and diaconal services, and to translate their enduring teachings about justice, freedom, peace, and benevolence into powerful new platforms for fostering public and private morality.

Much of the West has thus seen religious influences reemerge in all sorts of spaces and spheres of activity once seemingly closed to religion – in the services available in state schools, hospitals, and prisons; in the debates of state legislatures, courts, and tribunals; and in the discourses of human rights, public policy, and public health. Indeed, Western public life and political debates on many issues have become newly infused with religious metaphors, values, beliefs, and frameworks – sometimes hidden, sometimes syncretized, sometimes subsumed under other labels, but all of critical importance to community identity, integrity, and functioning. Moreover, many once distinctly church-based convictions and theologically loaded ethical commitments have shifted to other civil society associations and organizations, where they are having a beneficial effect – often with loosened but still persistent religious motives and attitudes. In some cases, these civil organizations cooperate with church diaconal and charitable institutions; in other cases, religious and civil forces are arrayed against each other.

Religion as a Differentiated Sphere in Late Modern Societies

Jürgen Habermas has argued that late modern pluralistic societies are "capitalist democracies ... that have remained susceptible to the erosion of their normative substance to this day as a result of the imperatives of capital's self-valorization."[60] While acknowledging this risk, our team of interdisciplinary scholars of religion has also found that ample "normative substance" remains in place in many late modern pluralistic societies, as do other moral "imperatives" that go beyond "self-valorization."[61] Our team has not offered a full-bodied song of praise for late modern pluralism, and several authors have raised skepticism about the role of religious institutions and of "structured pluralism" altogether in modern character formation. Worthy of note as well is the recent upheaval of liberal democratic conditions and the rise of authoritarian, even dictatorial politics in many Western countries. That authoritarian turn has featured not only the suppression of free speech and free press and new political manipulations of the legal system and scientific research. It has also often elevated and reenergized monohierarchical, patriarchal, and gerontocratic forms of

---

[60] Habermas, *Auch eine Geschichte der Philosophie*, 2:797.
[61] Michael Welker, John Witte, Jr., and Stephen Pickard, eds., *The Impact of Religion on Character Formation, Ethical Education, and the Communication of Values in Late Modern Pluralistic Societies* (Leipzig: Evangelische Verlagsanstalt, 2020) [hereafter *Religion and Character*].

religion in many quarters, not least in politics and in family life. These recent shifts have made it even more difficult today to demonstrate the effectiveness of "religion and faith as the basis of a free society",[62] and to parry charges that religion hinders or even prevents the pursuit of freedom, truth, and justice. For many critics, the recent resurgence of religion in Western lands is a danger to liberty and a threat to democracy.

In response, our research team has combined biblical, traditional, and modern interdisciplinary religious perspectives to press for constructive new relationships among the spheres of religion, law, and politics, and to offer a critical and self-critical appreciation of the authority of religion in and among many other social spheres. One of us (Michael Welker) examines the formative forces of Christian religion that is theologically oriented in terms of content.[63] He first critically examines the widespread forms of liberal piety and theology in the West that have contributed to the church's dwindling phenomena. This liberal piety has not retained or developed a rich sense of the creativity and richness of God or an awareness of God's spirit and the divine powers that sustain, save, judge, elevate, and exalt people. Liberal piety focuses on a human religious spirit that is usually understood in an individualistic and mentalistic way. This humanistic spirit is concentrated on a vaguely numinous transcendence or on very simple, almost empty thoughts of God, images of God, and feelings of God.

A biblically oriented knowledge of the divine spirit, on the other hand, can protect us from these empty, boring, and implausible concepts of God with their talk of abstract "omnipotence." The *divine spirit of justice, freedom, truth, peace, philanthropy, and love of neighbor* is a true powerhouse of goodness. It works in the complicated real world, which in many respects is certainly filled with good natural and cosmic forces, but also with many opposing destructive forces. This divine spirit does not become effective through abstract incantations of "religion and morality." It is not the private property of religions and morals. However, it opens many bridges to and sources of strength in other institutions and organizations in pluralistic society: to law, politics, science, education, the family, and health care.

The complex separation of powers in pluralistic societies, including the differentiation of the sphere of religion, is therefore not a decadent sign of the decline of late modernity, as many conservative political and religious voices claim. It is a source of strength for the preservation of the values of justice, freedom, truth, peace, humanity, and the protection and preservation of the forces of nature.

---

[62] See Paul Kirchhof, *Religion und Glaube als Grundlage einer freien Gesellschaft* (Munich: Herder, 2023).

[63] Michael Welker, "Consolation, Freedom, Justice, and Truth: Christian Religion, Character Formation, and Communication of Values", in *Religion and Character*, 29–39.

Not only theological but also anthropological reasons speak for the appreciation of a pluralistic ethos. German theologian Gregor Etzelmüller emphasizes this in his contribution.⁶⁴ He underscores how important it is to shift the focus from a fixation on natural evolution to a concentration on cultural evolution, without abandoning empirical and scientific observations. Studies of early childhood development provide rich material for appreciating transitions and interactions between natural and cultural processes. Moral and religious orientations play an important role in these developmental spurts in childhood, when connections between religious ethos, family ethos, neighborhood ethos, and a combination of principles of justice and protection of the weak are cultivated. Children are shaped in many ways by the creative forces of the divine spirit.

While Michael Welker and Gregor Etzelmüller encourage us to discover the theological and empirical-anthropological foundations of an ethos of pluralistic societies, American religious philosopher William Schweiker sheds light on the way pluralism also draws heavily on a secular ethical perspective.⁶⁵ He emphasizes that religious and moral communications are not necessarily good from the outset. Rather, theology and theological ethics must engage critically and constructively with religious interpretations of reality and with specific concepts of values. Virtue ethics has played a major role in this tradition. It has connected entire networks of values. However, it has often deceptively propagated the isomorphic view of the character and soul of the individual and the social community.

The ethos of pluralism demands a critical distance from such isomorphism. Schweiker pleads for a "Christian humanism" that opposes all dreams of totalitarian orientations and critically confronts all recommendations of metadiscourses and metanarratives. A differentiated defense of individual human dignity and the common good, which must always be redefined, should provide orientation. These concepts must confront many forms of "system paternalism", in Habermas's apt phrase, including its religious and antireligious varieties. And they must see that respect for human dignity does not end in an assertion of mere human autonomy.⁶⁶

---

⁶⁴ Gregor Etzelmüller, "Anthropology and Religious Formation", in *Religion and Character*, 41–52.
⁶⁵ William Schweiker, "Should Religion Shape Character?" in *Religion and Character*, 73–83.
⁶⁶ Peter Carnley, "The Fallacy of 'Individual Autonomy', and Moral Value in the Community of Christ", in *Religion and Character*, 63–71.

Several other contributors to our project echo these constructive and, at the same time, religiously and morally critical objections.[67] German systematic theologian Friederike Nüssel shows that ecumenical discourse in global Christianity has very hesitantly, but ultimately successfully, incorporated talk of values into theological language – even "values of the Gospel" and "values of the Kingdom of God."[68] Nüssel argues that this "values talk" has included a concentration on justice, peace, and the protection of the natural environment, even what might be boldly called the "integrity of creation." These ecumenical pronouncements promote not only understanding among different denominations but also the formation of communities of values and common promotion of justice, freedom, and peace, as well as the pursuit of tolerance, participation, and solidarity. Such ecumenical developments are cautiously influencing broader moral, legal, and political developments in Europe and far beyond.

The contributions by the South African scholar Piet Naudé and the Australian bishop Stephen Pickard also shed light on this promotion of justice and freedom in primarily political-critical and economic-critical perspectives. Naudé first shows how the globally influential theology of the leading Swiss theologian Karl Barth was criticized in South Africa in order to defend the theological underpinnings of apartheid.[69] Naudé then explains how Barth's theology was, in turn, also used by theologians in resistance to apartheid and in defense a modern pluralistic society, a constitution based on law and justice, and an enlightened value system. Finally, he explains how not only the profound theological, moral, and ethical insights of Dirk Smit and Gustavo Gutierrez, but also the philosophical, legal, economic, and economic-critical insights of John Rawls and Joseph Stiglitz came together in successful and influential proclamations against apartheid.

Anglican theologian and church leader Stephen Pickard also points in the direction of theological renewal as a corrective to social, cultural, and political developments.[70] He also begins with critical and self-critical perspectives on the church and culture, along with sober perceptions of a global development shaped by the modern Enlightenment and widespread antireligious resentment. He identifies a scientific naturalism and a "growth mantra" in modern pluralistic cultures that affects many other areas of life – education, health care, and reli-

---

[67] See Bernd Oberdorfer following Friedrich Schleiermacher: "'*With* Religion, not *from* Religion': Christian Antimoralist Moralism and Its Impact on Moral Formation", in *Religion and Character*, 217–24.

[68] Friederike Nüssel, "Values of the Gospel", in *Religion and Character*, 53–62.

[69] Piet Naudé, "The Impact of Religion on Shaping Values in Pluralistic Societies", in *Religion and Character*, 187–203.

[70] Stephen Pickard, "Optimal Environments for the Formation of Character", in *Religion and Character*, 205–15.

gion especially, alongside religion. He asks to what extent a "postsecular church" and the search for the common good in pluralistic societies can lead us out of the difficult situations we find ourselves in. In his view, the classic virtues of the Australian Anglican Church (commitment to welfare, social justice, and education) can be consolidated and renewed only through a committed theological and spiritual reorientation. He calls this "a recovery of the church" in "recovering a pace, rhythm, and presence in step with Christ."

English theologian Martyn Percy, in a contribution he calls "homiletic", warns against overpersonalizing problems of precarious political and economic dominance. He sheds light on the seemingly paradoxical connections between personal humility and the entrepreneurial will to create.[71] In doing so, he draws on the ideas of management expert Jim Collins, "one of the most important thought leaders in the corporate world." Percy illustrates his approach with biblical texts, well-known literature by Charles Dickens and Arthur Miller, and, above all, personal experiences and career path. For Christians, Percy argues, God's revelation in Jesus Christ opens their eyes to the transformation of ideas of omnipotence and omniscience through God's self-abasement in the Incarnation. In religious, social, and economic-professional practice, this ethos of humility leads to kindness and goodness, as well as to a cultural philanthropy. This human kindness is infectious. And this infectious human kindness is the sum of all thoughts and recommendations on the subject at hand: character development, ethical education, and communication of values – not only in pluralistic societies.

Critical Perspectives on the Project

Several contributors also raised fundamental criticisms about our project. American theologian Jennifer Herdt argues that while "there are negative lessons to learn from Max Weber's understanding of the differentiation of social spheres", that there are also "positive lessons to take from the longstanding Christian doctrine of the orders of creation, with its roots in natural law discourse."[72] Contrary to Christian critics of the doctrine of natural law, including Oliver O'Donovan and Michael Welker, Herdt emphasizes the blessing of the "dialectic of religious coinage" in diverse expressions of religious and ecclesiastical life. She has in mind the infinitely multicolored "plurality" of individual and social life in Western late modern societies, which she rightly wants to de-

---

[71] Martyn Percy, "Humility, Humiliation, and Hope: An Extended Homily on the Crucible for Authentic Character in Leadership", in *Religion and Character*, 171–84.

[72] Jennifer Herdt, "The Dialectic of Religious Formation", in *Religion and Character*, 85–99.

fend against a multisystemic structural or institutional pluralism. She emphasizes the great importance of open dialogical communication in everyday contexts and its formative, fluid influence on character development, ethical formation, and communication of values in late modern societies.

This perspective of open social plurality, in contrast to pluralism with its limited number of systems, was something we have not sufficiently considered when planning this major research project. The great importance of the plurality of many individuals became clear to us only when we became aware of more and more recent autocratic developments in various countries, which initially suppressed the free media, curbed the free expression of diverse public opinion with blackmail and prison sentences, and harassed civil society and the legal system. Our interest in distinguishing a "structured pluralism" – which was recognized not only by Max Weber but also by other important sociologists and social and cultural theorists – from a diffuse "plurality" of individual and social communication was indeed too one-sided. This made it even more important to our project to hear Jennifer Herdt, and other critical voices, including those from non-Christian traditions.

Israeli poet and Talmudic professor Admiel Kosman reinforces Herdt's reservations about pluralistic thinking in the spirit of great sociologists such as Max Weber, Talcott Parsons, and Niklas Luhmann.[73] Kosman recommends a focus on the thinking of Martin Buber and thus on so-called personalist or dialogist thinking. All perceptions and insights, he argues, must pass through the unique personality of the observing person, whether in scientific research or with unbiased common sense. To gain knowledge of the truth or of fundamental ethical guidelines, we must all go through the "everyday flow of life" and at the same time seek an encounter with the "spirit of the eternal you." Martin Buber recommends striving for a "loving science", a true philosophy as a loving philosophy that opens us up to "the unconditional mystery that we encounter in every sphere of our lives." In this encounter, every person can become a vessel for the resting of the spirit; in this encounter every person can align themselves with the absolute and hear the voice of truth.

German-based legal scholar Raja Sakrani highlights problems from the Muslim experience.[74] She sheds light on the aim of religious socialization to pass on traditional values to future generations and the associated importance of intergenerational loyalty. These concerns lead to manifold tensions between the oft diffuse expectations of multicultural and multireligious environments in

---

[73] Admiel Kosman, "Buber vs. Weber: Future Sociological Research According to Buber's Proposal – The I-Thou Relationship in Scholarly Research", in *Religion and Character*, 103–22.

[74] Raja Sakrani, "How to Be a 'Good' Muslim in Europe?", in *Religion and Character*, 123–46.

pluralistic societies and the inertial forces of ethnocultural affiliation. The most important challenges are the controversial assessment of women's active participation in public life and the rights of an individually self-determined lifestyle. Sakrani also emphasizes the considerable tensions between perspectives on the powerful expansion of Islam throughout the world and the assessment of it as a "subculture" in many parts of Europe. A wealth of tensions between traditional and contemporary norms and worldviews, between values shaped by family and nation and those shaped by democracy and cosmopolitanism, necessitates difficult and often painful learning processes on many sides. It is not uncommon for these learning processes to fail, leading to dull resignation and occasionally to violent resistance.

> The dynamics of Islamic religious socialization in Europe are negotiated along at least four central axes: the transition in the religious transmission process through symbolism and rituals or practices; the problem of the search for new religious authority and the creation of new theological and juridical Islamic universities and institutes; the growing claim to gender identity for women through religion; and finally a new requirement for citizenship. As to the question of how to be a good Muslim today in the pluralistic societies of Europe, the answer will certainly be pending when the process of religious socialization reflects the socio-legal contours more clearly. Furthermore, one must be aware of the "integration paradox" that reflects the complexity of Muslims' everyday lives.[75]

Hong Kong scholars of religion Milton Wai-Yiu Wan and Renee Lai-Fan Ip also describe considerable tensions between the pronounced family ethos in traditional Chinese cultures and the huge developments of economic, social, and political life, as well as scientific and media globalization processes. They describe the range of biological and psychological foundations of moral character formation, the cultural and normative weight of the more than two-thousand-year-old tradition of education within Chinese families, and the sometimes competing roles of philosophical and theological education in the moral learning processes.[76] The combination of developing individual moral character and its associated virtues along with successfully establishing social relationships that value interdependence and cooperation are central to Chinese traditions. Psychological and religious resources for self-development are emphasized to promote understanding and discreet interaction but also to perfect self-control and individual willpower. The authors speak of behavioral leaps ("habit loops")

---

[75] Ibid., 146.
[76] Milton Wai-Yiu Wan and Renee Lai-Fan, "Chinese Family Education and Spiritual Intervention", in *Religion and Character*, 147–57.

that can lead to a spiritual victory over a "sinful nature" weakened by powerlessness.

Chinese theologian Waihang Ng offers a complex view of the voices of Chinese, Greek, and early Christian classics in moral education.[77] He sheds light on value networks of political and military striving for power, but also on the associated moral, aesthetic, and religious education. These values, he believes, could also inform and guide multisystemic interactions and conflicts in late modern societies. Ng focuses on Homer's *Iliad*, Luo Guanzhong's *Three Kingdoms: A Historical Novel*, and selected passages from the New Testament Gospels. In the *Iliad*, he is captivated by the interplay of anger, defense of honor, and inevitable fate. The Chinese classic *Three Kingdoms* is about the advocacy or rejection of revenge, heavenly providence, and higher duties of justice and selfless friendship versus the pursuit of calculation and success. Ng contrasts these values and value conflicts with the Gospels' statements about anger and wrath, especially in Matthew and Mark. Inspired by the Heidelberg New Testament scholar Gerd Theißen, Ng emphasizes the importance of the early Christian development of an "aristocratic ethos" that overcomes anger and wrath in order to uplift fellow human beings and encourage them to behave in a way that is conducive to life. He attaches great importance to the interdependence of ethical and aesthetic impulses from literary and religious traditions, which can take up familial ethical, social, political, and even military development trends and transform them beneficially in educational processes.

Justice, Mercy, and Faith in Pluralist Context

From a completely different direction, German systematic theologian Philipp Stoellger questions the very intention of our whole project,[78] including understanding the role of religion and the church in influencing the formation of public or private morality in late modern pluralistic societies. Stoellger argues that the project depends upon an "outdated model" that assumes theology can explain what members of a church or a public should recognize, accept, and follow in their respective lives. He sees a "will to power" at work in many modern social spheres, which in the case of religion very easily reveals the sad picture of the search for relevance in a time of diminished public recognition and resonance. Stoellger recommends instead a "metaethical" approach that develops an "ethos of passions and fruitful passivities" in an effort to follow Christ. Jesus Christ was not a creator of values and a representative of values, he ar-

---

[77] Waihang Ng, "Literary Form, Paideia, and Religion", in *Religion and Character*, 159–69.
[78] Philipp Stoellger, "Formation as Figuration: The Impact of Religion Framed by Media Anthropology", in *Religion and* Character, 225–35.

gues. But Jesus showed a unique "passion for the neighbor", which provides the soft "medial power" that surrounds and "frames" all human activities, a power that God reveals in Jesus Christ and in his Spirit.

It is certainly appropriate to warn against trumping or "gotcha" gestures and a triumphalist "will to power" in a large-scale project that aims to investigate the circulation of influences and the formation of value hierarchies in late modern pluralistic societies. However, it is also appropriate to warn against a kind of "reverse trump" project, which can easily encourage a mysticism of suffering under the keywords "passion" and "passivity." One could speak of two models of "framing" in the search for a fruitful framework for individual and social existence in the religious and political present. The insistence on a strict theological orientation toward the suffering and crucified Jesus Christ does indeed seem to speak in favor of the reverse-trump model, but this would offer only very cloudy perspectives on the social conditions surrounding theology.

A theological orientation toward the crucified and risen Christ in the power of his Spirit "poured out" on his witnesses – which is also a spirit of justice, freedom, truth, human kindness, and peace[79] – must deal with the accusation of an intentionally triumphalist theology. It must learn to deal critically and self-critically with the dangers of a self-righteous ethos of humanity. What Stoellger calls an "outdated model" is, in fact, an ethos that is not only grounded Christologically, biblically, and theologically but also spiritually founded beyond the scope of Christian religion and churches. It is also about "the weightier matters of the law: justice, mercy, and pistis (faith and worship)" (Matthew 23:23). The first and last two contributions in this volume deal with these major topics, which have been relevant for thousands of years and are still highly topical today.

German practical theologian Johannes Eurich uses selected examples to describe the development of organized diaconal aid for the poor, disadvantaged, and sick in Europe since the nineteenth century.[80] He shows how those receiving and giving help sought not only to improve their performance but also to gain a deeper understanding of the connections between physical illness and mental and spiritual needs. In line with more recent developments in the exchange of theological, sociopolitical, medical, and scientific studies, the physical condition of the human being and of human cognition has taken center stage. This reorientation has influenced not only organized diaconal and charitable institutions in Germany and beyond, but also theological ethics, biblical exegesis, and practical and pastoral theological education. Eurich shows the importance

---

[79] Michael Welker, *In the Image of God: An Anthropology of the Spirit* (Grand Rapids: Eerdmans, 2021).

[80] Johannes Eurich, "Learning to Care for the Whole Person: The Significance of Body and Soul for Diaconal Work", *Religion and Character*, 237–60.

of intensified perceptions of the physical dimensions not only of human well-being but also of human dignity, suffering, and death. This must also be conveyed in educational processes and in political and legal design concerns, he argues. A constructive and critical examination of economic and media interests in the body as the primary medium of human self-presentation and a pronounced cult of the body is just as necessary as psychological and medical skills in dealing with the vulnerability and fragility of the human body and human life.

One of us (John Witte, Jr.) concludes our study by focusing on the legal sphere, and the historical development and continued values of the doctrine of the "threefold use of the law."[81] This "uses" doctrine, he shows, has roots in biblical traditions and in early Christian and medieval theologies, but it came to new prominence in the Protestant Reformation. The reformers differentiated the civil, theological, and educational uses of the moral law of God and the positive laws and normative regimes of states, churches, and even in families, schools, and other social spheres. Witte shows how the uses-of-law doctrine was further developed in the centuries following the Reformation and how they are still unquestionably important today in the "development of character, ethical formation, and communication of values" not only in late modern pluralistic societies. He develops this argument very concretely using the example of contemporary criminal law and punishment, whose main purposes of deterrence, retribution, and rehabilitation echo if not express the civil, theological, and educational uses of the law. Fruitful relationships between religious and theological traditions and contemporary lawmaking can be observed here, with many repercussions on moral and political conditions. Late modern societies also need these numerous spillover effects to cultivate and maintain the values and virtues that are often important to them and not infrequently vital in practice.

---

[81] John Witte, Jr., "The Uses of Law for the Formation of Character: A Classic Protestant Doctrine for Late Modern Liberal Societies?" in *Religion and Character*, 261–83.

Chapter 3

Politics and the State

Political Forms and Moral Formation

In its most basic sense, politics is the activity of governing a discrete people and territory. Historically in the West, those who governed came to their positions by conquest, custom, or consent, or by inheritance, election, or appointment. Some polities were organized as monarchies, some as oligarchies, some as democracies, most a mixture of the three. Political officials could be emperors, monarchs, or dukes; popes, bishops, or abbots; tribal chieftains, manorial princes, or feudal lords. Their regimes ranged from extended households to bishoprics, tribal lands, cities, nations, and empires. Whatever their origin, organization, and orbit of influence, political officials in the West have generally engaged in a common set of activities that constitute the heart of politics. They protect and preserve the community and its welfare; make and enforce law; broker and resolve disputes; punish crime and civil offenses; negotiate diplomacy; collect taxes; raise armies; wage war; and engage in numerous activities that are necessary and proper to the political office and that ideally serve the common good.

To be effective and enduring, political activity classically required a balance of the political virtues and attributes of power, authority, coercion, persuasion, piety, charisma, justice, equity, clemency, courage, moderation, temperance, force, faithfulness, and more. The moral character and ethical example of political rulers have long been important criteria of good government in Western lands, producing a millennia-long cottage industry of "mirrors" and manuals designed to educate each ruler on the exemplary character traits and moral standing that become the political office. Part of that moral education of the political ruler came from religious officials who have long been essential political allies; at their best, they lent sanctity, legitimacy, and pageantry to the political office as well as counsel, comfort, and commodities to political officials. While some religious leaders still play that political educational role today, the popular press and broader media together with economic and lobbying forces now have a far more decisive influence on the moral character of political rulers who are chosen for office.

Today, almost all late modern pluralistic nations are organized as democratic states, although some of them have attendant constitutional monarchies with limited jurisdiction. Almost all Western governments have reduced the formal role of religion and the church in daily political life, although some nations still have concordats with the Vatican, clergy in their legislatures, and formal state establishments that support Christian clergy, churches, schools, and charities. Most Western nations have written constitutions, charters, or comparable organic acts that define in detail the powers and provinces of political authorities and that govern the sometimes-fraught moments of political reform, transition, or expansion. Most Western nations now make formal distinctions among the executive, legislative, and judicial powers of government and functions of law, each designed in part to check and balance the other. Most have sophisticated rules and procedures to facilitate the legal transactions and interactions of their citizens and subjects; to protect public, private, penal, and procedural rights; and to resolve disputes between and among citizens and political authorities. Most recognize multiple sources of law and political power – constitutions, treaties, statutes, regulations, judicial precedents, customary practices, and a growing body of private and public international laws.

Beyond the positive or negative moral examples and charisma of state officials, the modern state affects and effects the people's character formation, ethical education, and the communication of values in a variety of ways. This moral formation comes through the state's many "thou shalt" commands ("pay your taxes"; "educate your children"; "register your properties") and "thou shalt not" commands ("do not kill", "do not steal", "do not bear false witness"). It comes through its formal state-run systems of education from kindergarten to university, and its less formal but pervasive instructions about private and public health, safety, and welfare. It comes through the teachings, practices, symbols, ceremonies, and statuary of state-established or -supported churches, schools, and charities.

This moral education also comes through the myriad ways that state policies and procedures nudge, encourage, incentivize, and facilitate citizens to adopt certain behaviors and avoid others. Tax deductions encourage marriage, charity, and home ownership. Heavy license fees and taxes discourage smoking and drinking. Zoning, land use, and nuisance laws guide the appropriate uses of properties. Civil rights laws encourage more inclusive employment decisions and public accommodations. Same-sex marriage rights invite a more expansive understanding of domestic relations. Education licenses define the baseline content of public and private schools. Rather like trees and plants bending to the light, both individuals and nonstate institutions often position and incline their moral choices and habits to enjoy the benefits of state policies – and sometimes contort or camouflage themselves to avoid the political shadows.

Modern Politics in Interdisciplinary Perspective

Given its perennial prominence in society and its vast coercive power and potential for being and doing good or evil, the modern state has attracted a massive body of interdisciplinary scholarship. Some of that scholarship has been bundled into the discrete fields of political theory, political science, comparative politics, international relations, public administration, political theology, political ethics, political psychology, and sundry more focused studies of individual national or regional governments or of political activities like elections or policymaking. Some of that scholarship takes place in other fields of study – say, law, sociology, or history – that focus on the state or politics as a discrete theme.

Our international research team that took up this vast topic comprised sociologists, philosophers, ethicists, lawyers, and economists, led by South African polymath Piet Naudé.[82] Their work provided different windows of critical reflection on the impact of the modern state on character formation, ethical education, and the communication of values in late modern pluralistic societies. We offer a few samples of their work here, focused especially on a few of the dangerous and contested points of inquiry.

In a critical study, South African political scientist Amanda Gouws argues that the success of modern pluralistic societies has long depended on an underappreciated "ethics of care", in leading feminist Carol Gilligan's apt phrase.[83] Modern pluralistic societies work because a large portion of the population – disproportionately women – are raised to feel duty-bound to provide essential services such as child-rearing, elder care, household management, and emotional labor. The state is efficient, Gouws writes, and "the market is 'free' because women do the unpaid care work that sustains a free-market economy."[84] (One could say the same thing about the voluntary services of churches, charities, and philanthropies, which still provide much essential labor and capital that often go unheralded and unheeded.) Nonetheless, the dominant political narrative of neoliberalism still praises liberty, equality, autonomy, and self-determina-

---

[82] Piet Naudé, Michael Welker, and John Witte, Jr., eds., *The Impact of Political Economy on Character Formation, Ethical Education, and the Communication of Values in Late Modern Pluralistic Societies* (Leipzig: Evangelische Verlagsanstalt, 2023) [hereafter *Political Economy and Character*.

[83] Amanda Gouws, "Neoliberal Political Economy and Value Transmission: What We Can Learn from Feminist Care Ethics", in *Political Economy and Character*, 31–44.

[84] Ibid., 38.

tion, often coupled with old traditions of sexism. Liberalism prioritizes the individual over the collective and emphasizes transactional living, all the while neglecting the voluntary delivery of essential services by vast portions of the population. As this ethos of liberalism spreads, it deprecates values that cannot be monetized, and reinforces power imbalances that often disadvantage marginalized groups, women especially. Gouws argues that modern pluralistic societies have much to learn from an "ethics of care" that prizes values that are relational and voluntary, not transactional and monetized. A political ethic of solidarity, care, and the common good, Gouws argues, holds much more promise than the false political promises and platitudes of many modern pluralistic societies.

American sociologist Andreas Glaeser, too, criticizes the individualist emphasis of some modern theories of political liberalism.[85] All persons operate within a variety of institutional frameworks, Glaeser writes, which are themselves the product of specific histories and ongoing processes. In marked contrast to monopolistic, even tyrannical political regimes that inevitably fail, successful pluralistic societies have learned to value the integrity of the many social institutions that shape and are shaped by individual behavior. "Seeing humans as living in and through institutions shifts the focus of classical ethics away from individuals to larger social wholes. Kant's question, 'what ought *I* to do?' thus becomes, 'what assemblage of institutions ought *we* to form such that all citizens have more of an opportunity to act ethically in view of the myriad consequences of their actions on self, others and the environment?'"[86]

This kind of question demands deep engagement with the ethical impact and imprint of every social institution, not least the state, Glaeser insists. He posits three principles to guide this deep engagement: "transparency, alterability, and value conformity." Of the first principle, he writes: "Knowledge about the ways in which institutions transform actions into a plethora of consequences for their own self-maintenance, for the people who carry them, and for others merely affected by them is the condition sine qua non for political action." Political action, in turn, must be animated by alterability, a perennial desire to reform and improve not only the state, but all social institutions that are implicated in a morally compromised system. Such reform efforts, still further, require citizens to conform to certain values through the proper education, moral imagination, and "sociological knowledge to map out workable and effective actions plans." Finally, for this collective pan-institutional reform effort to be effective requires a pluralistic society with some shared social sense of what the good life in a good society looks like. While this ideal of an open and inclusive "civic ethos" is sometimes achieved in smaller communities, however, to-

---

[85] Andreas Glaeser, "Ethics' Political Imperative: Moving toward Better Institutions", in *Political Economy and Character*, 45–66.

[86] Ibid., 65.

day's modern pluralistic world is too often harmed by the "the logics of profit-seeking media and polarizing mobilizational politics" that trade in false facts, fictional narratives, and fixations on power accumulations, not justice, peace, and order.[87]

Reflecting in part this latter concern, Australian ethicist Jonathan Cole takes on the effect of Twitter (now known simply as X) and other social media not only in manipulating elections and other political processes, but also in eroding the vital personal interactions and political debates that are at the heart of deliberative democracies.[88] Cole notes that Twitter's design features – anonymity, brevity, interpolation, unmoderatability, and the invisibility of mitigating circumstances – each contribute to a decline in healthy conversations and the erosion of societal norms. To be sure, sometimes anonymity is critical for vital information to be shared: think of whistle-blowers, journalistic sources, witness-protection programs, security and intelligence services, and more. But a healthy democracy and a just government normally work best in an open marketplace of political ideas – where arguments can be proffered and challenged, facts can be asserted and verified, policies can be debated and adjusted. By contrast, Twitter and comparable social media uniquely combine various physical and analogue social systems into a single networked speech forum, spanning sports, entertainment, news, political activism, and social commentary. Twitter flattens and homogenizes all information from the trivial to the politically momentous and reduces it to short tweets. Moreover, it breeds toxicity and dishonesty by allowing users to engage anonymously in discussions that would typically require identification in other public forums like television, print media, public lectures, debates, or panel discussions. This is dangerous in an attention economy where views and engagement are monetized and thus prioritized over accuracy.

Italian sociologist Sergio Belardinelli also emphasizes the essential interplay between individuals and social structures in modern pluralistic societies and the need for continuous honest exchange between individual choice and social structures.[89] Each person is "a synthetic point of ... unrepeatable uniqueness", he writes. But at the same time, each person is the inevitable part and product of a "constitutive relationality" and a set of social contingencies and cultural conditions over which they have little choice. Modern liberal societies work best when they offer all citizens robust and holistic education "to help the new generation find its way, feel at home in the world we all live in, and

---

[87] Ibid., 52, 56, 64–65.
[88] Jonathan Cole, "Twitter: A Case-Study in the Character-Malformation Potential of Twenty-First-Century Digital Technology", in *Political Economy and Character*, 169–88.
[89] Sergio Belardinelli, "Social Systems, Moral Individualism, and Education", in *Political Economy and Character*, 101–14.

simply become what we are: people, free people, whose unrepeatable uniqueness is rooted in a network of foundational relationships that also encompasses our duties and responsibilities."[90] But sadly, higher education in many liberal lands has become too expensive for many, too specialized and narrowly focused on job creation, or too preoccupied with ideological fictions and fashions that provide little preparation for budding citizens and social leaders. Today, rather than teaching students the essential knowledge, moral norms, and social habits to navigate our complex world, education is becoming a means of bolstering the social capital of the already privileged.

Australian jurist Nicholas Aroney focuses on the interlocking roles of economics, law, education, and religion in shaping conceptions of a virtuous society under the dominant social imaginary of modern liberal democracy.[91] "Law regulates outward behavior, education informs inward beliefs, and economics provides our needs and satisfies our preferences", Aroney writes. Modern liberalism argues that these core social systems must be morally neutral and value free, leaving individuals to make those choices for themselves. But in a virtuous society, these social systems ultimately depend on some shared normative essence, some binding moral impulses, some core convictions about personal conduct and civic responsibility – all of which are uniquely provided by religion. The social spheres of economics, law, and education operate best in modern pluralistic societies when they "leave room for religion to perform its unique function" and when they interact productively with religious ideas and institutions. Rather than pretending that economics is value-neutral, it is better for a just society to recognize that markets require informed moral choices by buyers and sellers, and adequate moral guidance from public and private regulators. Rather than pretend that state laws are only the temporary commands of the current sovereign, it is better for a just government to build its laws on the deep moral and religious foundations of the legal tradition and to apply those laws with the justice, equity, and mercy that has long marked virtuous state rule. Rather than pretend that state-run schools can bracket religion from primary education, it is better for young students from the start to learn how to navigate religious pluralism and to learn about the religious sources and dimensions of the many subjects they are studying, not least politics and statecraft.

American constitutional lawyer Nathan Chapman underscores the complementary and complicated role of private religious schools in cultivating moral

---

[90] Ibid., 109.
[91] Nicholas Aroney, "Economics, Law, Education, and Religion – Contributions to the Composition of a Good Society", in *Political Economy and Character*, 81-100.

virtues in citizens and building a just society.[92] In the United States, "schools are a battleground ... because they implicate a liberal republic's interest in forming citizens", Chapman argues. Numerous court cases debate the respective roles of the state and parents in rearing children and in cultivating ethical values, moral practices, and religious beliefs in the next generation. Over the past century, the courts have effectively created a two-tiered educational system: public, state-run schools that forbid religious instruction, and private schools that are free to teach their distinct religious beliefs and moral values. While public schools are free, private schools have historically been cut off from public funding, and thus charge tuition that many students and families cannot afford. To reduce this inequity and to enhance educational choice, American courts have recently allowed some states funding for private religious schools. But states have begun to condition that funding on each school's adherence to nondiscrimination laws, particularly those that protect LGBTQ+ students and employees. Some American states, like their counterparts in Canada, have also begun to insist that private religious schools teach other core values of modern liberalism as a condition for state funding and sometimes accreditation. Private schools with religious and moral commitments to the contrary must now either forgo vital funding or face expensive lawsuits for discrimination. While not predicting the best constitutional solution, Chapman criticizes this as a false choice that undercuts modern liberalism's commitments to structural pluralism and private choice and America's distinct constitutional commitments to establishing no religion (whether sectarian or secular) and to protecting the religious freedom of all.

As a final illustration of different perspectives on politics and the state, one of us (John Witte) asks the loaded political, moral, and religious question: What happens when the state acts to malign a citizen's character, to violate their morality, to abridge their basic rights, to compel them to act or forgo action contrary to their conscience or faith?[93] Even worse, what happens when the state becomes an outright tyrant? When, how, and on what grounds may a citizen reject, resist, and even revolt against the state altogether or against individual state actors? These are perennial questions in the Western tradition, he shows, going back to biblical and classical sources, and they have produced a sizeable library of reflections over the centuries. But these questions remain the stuff of daily headlines today, not only in late modern liberal societies but indeed throughout the world. Just ask people in Ukraine, Hong Kong,

---

[92] Nathan S. Chapman, "Constitutional Rules and the Political Economy of Character Formation: Conditions on Government Aid to Religious Schools as a Case Study", in *Political Economy and Character,* 209–30.

[93] John Witte, Jr., "Resisting Political Authority to Protect Faith and Morality: Enduring Lessons from the Lutheran Reformation", in *Political Economy and Character,* 189–208.

Iran, Northern Africa, North Korea, the Philippines, Central America, and way too many other places around the world facing rogue and oppressive states or invading foreign powers.

When such political intrusions on liberty, morality, and conscience are lower, as they are in most late liberal societies today, oppressed citizens usually have "softer" force at their disposal to protect themselves – by filing for an injunction, pressing a lawsuit, lobbying for legal change, invoking checks and balances, issuing petitions and grievances, mobilizing shame through media exposures, disobeying or demonstrating as we have seen in recent campaigns in the United States against, say, gross racism and police brutality. But when the political intrusions on liberty and morality are graver, as they are and have been in too many parts of the world, oppressed citizens use "harder force." When citizens have no other legal recourse, they can resist and rejoin, even with violence, those who violate their faith, freedom, family, and other fundamentals. When the rule of law breaks, when oppression and tyranny break out, a whole community can resort to revolt, rebellion, and even organized revolution.

Modern liberal pluralistic societies in the West were born of this logic in the great democratic revolutions of the sixteenth to nineteenth centuries. New pluralistic societies in the Global South were born of the anticolonial and antiautocratic movements of the twentieth century. The new millennium has brought on powerful new challenges that are raising these questions anew and deeply testing and contesting fundamental political systems from within and from without. It is essential for modern pluralistic societies and states to get their own houses in order, and to strengthen the roles of all social institutions and citizens in the pursuit of liberty, justice, peace, order, and moral flourishing.

Chapter 4

Law and Justice

In its broadest sense, law consists of all the written and unwritten norms that govern human conduct – moral commandments, family rules, church canons, state statutes, commercial codes, communal customs, local conventions, and many others. All these laws on the books and in action help to shape the morality and character of persons and peoples – by encouraging and directing, prescribing and prohibiting, supporting and facilitating, rewarding and punishing, limiting and nudging their choices and conduct, relationships and institutions.[94]

In premodern societies, these sundry laws overlapped, as they were often enacted and enforced by interwoven religious, political, economic, feudal, and familial authorities.[95] In modern liberal societies, however, the state is a differentiated sphere, and its legal system is formally separated from the internal laws of nonstate associations. While the moral influence of modern state laws is our principal focus in this chapter, it is worth remembering that the internal laws of nonstate associations remain critical sources of moral formation and ethical education for individuals and groups today. A parent's order to their bickering children – "Stop fighting now!" – carries much more moral weight than the state criminal prohibitions on assault and battery. A church's rules about worship and liturgy shape religious and moral habits much more than the state's constitutional guarantees about religious freedom. The conduct codes of schools or workplaces offer far more pervasive moral direction for

---

[94] See generally, John Witte, Jr. and Michael Welker, eds., *The Impact of Law on Character Formation, Ethical Education, and the Communication of Values in Late Modern Pluralistic Societies* (Leipzig: Evangelische Verlagsanstalt, 2021) [hereafter *Law and Character*]. See further, Michael Welker and Gregor Etzelmüller, eds., *Concepts of Law in the Sciences, Legal Studies, and Theology* (Tübingen: Mohr Siebeck, 2013).

[95] Kenneth John Crispin, "Law, Values, and Moral Influence", in *Law and Character*, 263–78.

their members than state laws about education or labor relations. Ideally, in modern liberal societies the laws of the state support, not supplant, the internal laws of nonstate associations. Indeed, these nonstate laws are critical bulwarks of liberty and morality against an overreaching state legal system.

All modern liberal states are dedicated to the "rule of law" – to maintaining a *Rechtsstaat*.[96] Most modern states have written or unwritten constitutions that define the powers and provinces of political authorities and the rights and duties of their political subjects. Most separate the executive, legislative, and judicial powers of government and functions of law, and provide formal constitutional checks and balances against political abuse and legal overreach. Most distinguish public laws (governing officials and citizens), private laws (governing citizens and associations), penal laws (prohibiting crimes), and procedural laws (that allow the state to prosecute crimes and citizens to bring private lawsuits). Most modern legal systems recognize multiple sources and forms of law beyond constitutions: treaties, charters, covenants, concordats, statutes, regulations, cases, customs, conventions, and more. Of increasing importance in the past century have been international laws to deal with global legal issues: human rights violations, war, genocide, terrorism, arms trafficking, refugees, migrants, sex trafficking, disease, hunger, famine, poverty, failed states, political and economic corruption, global climate and environmental challenges, (bio)technological issues, and much more.

Today, modern liberal societies and their members depend upon such state laws to provide basic social order, peace, security, crime control, stable infrastructures, reliable markets, accountable government, peaceful transfers of power, elementary due process, fair judicial tribunals, and fundamental rights protections for individuals and groups.[97] Having this basic legal order in place is a precondition to human survival, let alone moral thriving. Aristotle said this already in his *Politics:* "Just as man is the best of the animals when completed, when separated from law and adjudication he is the worst of all."[98] James Madison made this same point two millennia later: "If men were angels, no [law or] government would be necessary. If angels were to govern men, neither external nor internal controls … would be necessary. In framing a government which is

---

[96] Patrick Parkinson, "Law, Morality, and the Fragility of the Western Legal Tradition", in *Law and Character*, 21–36.

[97] See, ibid.; Crispin, "Law, Values, and Moral Influence"; and further the recent overview in Gerald J. Postema, *Law's Rule: The Nature, Value, and Viability of the Rule of Law* (Oxford: Oxford University Press, 2022).

[98] Aristotle, *Politics*, bk. 1, chap. 2.

to be administered by men over men ... experience has taught mankind the necessity of auxiliary precautions."[99]

The issue has always been how far these "auxiliary precautions" of state law should go. After all, Western history is littered with grim examples of political tyranny, terrorism, and totalitarianism, with state laws and legal institutions used as sharp and sinister instruments of control, coercion, and brutality. Even in the past century, purportedly modern liberal states have sometimes directed their laws to support slavery, apartheid, genocide, colonialism, persecution, violence, racism, bigotry, intolerance, chauvinism, and many other shameful forms of moral failures and injustice at home and abroad. These proclivities to legal and political abuse have, at minimum, underscored the need for modern liberal societies to limit closely the roles and rules of state law and to protect zealously the rights and liberties of individuals and nonstate institutions.

These proclivities have led modern scholars like German philosopher Rüdiger Bittner to challenge the very notion that state law can serve as any kind of moral teacher for modern pluralistic societies. Not only are our modern society's morals too variant to select one form of morality for coercive legal enforcement by the state, Bittner argues. But the state simply cannot be trusted to do more than maintain the legal minima to keep basic social order. Haven't we learned anything from the Nazi, Communist, and Fascist regimes of the twentieth century, or the scary new forms of political belligerence on the far right and far left that have broken out on both sides of the Atlantic? We need fewer, not more state laws, Bittner concludes, and those laws should focus only on discharging the core responsibilities of statecraft, not interfering in the moral formation of citizens.[100]

These skeptical views about state power and law are popular today among various libertarians, neo-Anabaptists, and neo-Augustinians (Augustine had famously called for just enough laws to control a "den of robbers").[101] Some libertarians today thus call for the end of the modern welfare state, the truncation of government bureaucracy, the decriminalization of all but deeply harmful conduct, and the reprivatization of much of public and private life that state laws have gradually come to govern over the past century. Some Anabaptists and neo-Augustinians, dismayed by what they regard as the growing immorality of modern state laws, have echoed Catholic philosopher Alasdair McIntyre's

---

[99] James Madison, *Federalist No. 51*, in Clinton Rossiter, ed., *The Federalist Papers: Alexander Hamilton, James Madison, John Jay* (New York: American Library, 1961), 320–25, at 322.

[100] Rüdiger Bittner, "The Law as Educator", in *Law and Character*, 83–94.

[101] Quoted and discussed in Jean Bethke Elshtain, "There Oughta Be a Law About This – Not Necessarily: The Limits of Law as a Teacher of Values and Virtues", in *Law and Character*, 67–82, at 69. See further ibid., 80–82.

proposal for a "Benedict option" that ascetically separates Christian communities as far as possible from the state and its laws.[102] Some legal scholars have called for stronger "faith-based" legal systems that allow religious authorities more autonomy to govern the family, education, charity, inheritance, zoning, labor, policing, and other legal needs of their voluntary faithful without state interference.[103]

Other scholars, like American philosophers Brian Bix and Jean Bethke Elshtain, have warned about the ample "moral slippage" that can occur when the state attempts to legislate and enforce too much morality. They allow that criminal laws, rigorously enforced, might produce better behavior by criminals but rarely better morals, since prison often erodes a convict's morality. But the more the state tries to assume the role of moral educator in society, these authors argue, the more it threatens the roles and rules of older, often more effective local seats of moral authority like families, churches, neighborhoods, and voluntary associations – and the more it threatens to erode each citizen's incentive to develop an ethic of "self-help, personal involvement", and moral investment in their communities. The more we grow accustomed to the state discharging our family's, our church's, or our personal moral obligations to God, neighbor, and self – think of the massively disaffected workers in the Soviet Union or state-established churches sitting empty like mausoleums – the more we lose our moral autonomy, agency, capacity, and incentive. Sometimes, too, a new state law enacted for seemingly good reasons of "public health, safety, and morality" – think of stay-at-home or mask mandates in response to COVID – can trigger deliberate disobedience and organized resistance by some citizens, further eroding public and private morality in so doing.[104]

These are wise caveats that underscore the necessarily limited role that state law can play in moral formation and ethical education in modern pluralistic societies with multiple institutions, each with its own moral and legal systems. But we think there is enduring wisdom in ancient Greek philosopher Xenophilos's remark, echoed by Hegel, that "the best way to educate people is to

---

[102] Alasdair McIntryre, *After Virtue: A Study in Moral Theory* (Notre Dame, IN: University of Notre Dame Press, 1981), 263. See expansion of this idea in Rod Dreher, *The Benedict Option: A Strategy for Christians in a Post-Christian* (New York: Sentinel, 2017), albeit with criticisms from MacIntyre here: https://tradistae.com/2020/04/21/macintyre-benop/.

[103] See critical analysis in John Witte, Jr., *Church, State, and Family: Reconciling Traditional Teachings and Modern Liberties* (Cambridge: Cambridge University Press, 2019), 300–35.

[104] See Elshtain, "There Oughta Be a Law" and Brian Bix, "The Effects of (Family) Law: Frameworks, Practical Reasoning, Social Norms, and Slippage", in *Law and Character*, 53–67.

make them citizens of a city with good laws."[105] And we think there is enduring wisdom in St. Paul's teaching, developed anew by American ethicist and jurist Cathleen Kaveny, that "the law was our schoolmaster (*paidagōgos*) until Christ came."[106] Yes, Christ and the spiritual founders and prophets of other religious traditions do provide people of faith with a higher spiritual morality than any state law can or should provide. Even so, the law of the modern state does and can provide people of all faiths or no faith with social stability and ethical education that fosters a kind of baseline "civil morality." This can be seen in several examples from across modern legal systems.

First, the criminal laws of the modern state echo and enforce many traditional moral teachings. Every modern state law has variations on ancient "thou shalt" and "thou shalt not" commands, which they back with criminal sanctions: Do not kill. Do not steal. Do not bear false witness. Do not covet or violate your neighbor's household. Do not rape, assault, batter, or kidnap your neighbor. Do not commit incest, bestiality, polygamy, and other sex crimes. Nurture your children. Repay your debts. Honor your promises. Respect the authorities. Pay your taxes. Register your properties. Answer your conscriptions. Obey the court's orders. Modern penal codes in liberal lands are filled with such commandments. They are reminder claims of our basic moral duties, normative guard rails to keep us roughly on course.[107]

Through its published penal codes and public prosecution of offenders, and through the publicity of its punishments and criminal records, the criminal law of the modern state teaches some of the basic values of civil morality. The criminal law system further affirms the moral agency of each rational person, and their duties and rights of moral desert. It communicates the essential duties of all to respect the body, property, interests, and reputation of their neighbors. It commands everyone to honor the legitimate authorities of the state in their administration and enforcement of the law – provided those authorities, too, respect the basic rights and liberties of each defendant. Ideally, state criminal laws also can help to form and reform the character and basic morality of duly convicted criminals – forcing them to confront and ideally confess their guilt, making them pay for their violations of the community's norms and the victim's well-being, and rehabilitating them through teaching

---

[105] Diogenes Laërtius, *Vitae* VIII.16 and G. W. F. Hegel, *Grundlinien der Philosophie des Rechts*, ed. J. Hoffmeister, 4th ed. (Berlin: Meiner, 1955), §153, at p. 143. Quoted by Bittner, "The Law as Educator", 85–86, although Bittner ultimately rejects this proposition.

[106] See Ephesians 3:24 and discussion in Cathleen Kaveny, "Law's Pedagogy in a Pluralistic Society: Challenges and Opportunities", in *Law and Character*, 37–52.

[107] See Mark Hill et al., eds., *Christianity and Criminal Law* (London: Routledge, 2020).

or reteaching the basic norms of sociability and good citizenship that they must demonstrate to reenter society.[108]

Second, between and beyond these apodictic poles of thou shalt and thou shalt not commands, the modern liberal state often operates with softer and more subtle methods of encouraging and facilitating preferred moral behavior and discouraging or impeding immoral behavior. "Nudging" is what behavioral scientists call this common legal strategy of promoting desirable public and private goods in many areas of life.[109] Particularly in its vast network of regulatory laws, the modern liberal state commends, licenses, and sometimes even pays for or rewards all kinds of morally desirable behavior. Think of getting a license to marry or to open a business, voting or running in a state election, getting a free vaccine or medical procedure, going to college on a state scholarship. In turn, the state imposes taxes or fines or withholds state benefits or opportunities for those who indulge in morally undesirable behavior: think of smoking, not wearing seat belts, dropping out of school, or not paying child support. The theory of nudging stipulates that, over time, the desirable behavior encouraged by the state will become more customary, even natural or reflexive among citizens, and the undesirable behavior will be viewed as aberrant and perhaps even stigmatized.

Third, modern constitutional laws – on the books and in action – foster moral values and ethical education about good government, good citizenship, and good neighborliness. Think of the powerful new European constitutions enacted after World War II – starting with the Basic Law of Germany (1949) with its striking moral and communal premises:

> Conscious of their responsibility before God and man. Inspired by their determination to promote world peace as an equal partner in a unified Europe, the German people, in the exercise of their constituent power [declare:] ... (1) Human dignity shall be inviolable. To respect and protect it shall be the duty of all state authority. (2) The German people therefore acknowledge inviolable and inalienable human rights as the basis of every community, of peace and of justice in the world.[110]

---

[108] See further John Witte, Jr., "Teaching Sexual Morality in Church and State: Historically and Today", in *Law and Character*, 193–214; and John Witte, Jr., "The Uses of Law for the Formation of Character: A Classic Protestant Doctrine for Late Modern Liberal Societies?" in Michael Welker et al., eds., *The Impact of Religion on Character Formation in Late Modern Societies* (Leipzig: Evangelische Verlagsanhalt, 2020) [hereafter *Religion and Character*], 261–83.

[109] Richard H. Thaler and Cass R. Sunstein, *Nudge: The Final Edition* (New York: Penguin, 2021); see other legal examples in Witte, *Church, State, and Family*, 209–11.

[110] See https://www.gesetze-im-internet.de/englisch_gg/englisch_gg.html with discussion in Ute Mager, "The German Constitution as Value System", in *Law and Character*, 164–75.

Think of the powerful human rights documents that now govern modern liberal societies – the European Convention on Human Rights (1950), the American Civil Rights Act (1964), the Canadian Charter of Rights and Freedoms (1982), the United Kingdom Human Rights Act (1998), and many others that detail the rights and liberties that all persons and institutions deserve.[111] Think of the landmark cases in many high courts in Western lands – like *Brown v. Board of Education* (1954) and *Obergefell v. Hodges* (2015) in the United States that sought to end racism and homophobia.[112] Think of constitutional religious freedom guarantees that not only enable individuals to enjoy freedom of conscience and free exercise of religion, but also allow faith communities to incorporate themselves as religious bodies, to govern their own property, polity, and personnel, to set their own doctrine, liturgy, and discipline, to gather for worship, education, and catechesis, to build and operate schools, seminaries, charities, hospitals, and relief centers that cater to the public and private good.[113] Think of state education laws that help habituate the next generation of citizens in the basic values of democratic citizenship, with state schools sometimes teaching more expansive ethical habits of democratic citizenry and private religious schools sometimes fostering the moral formation of a child in a particular faith.[114] Think of more prosaic but essential constitutionally protected taxation laws that facilitate various forms and forums of distributive justice of wealth and resources to those who need more.[115]

South African theologian Dirkie Smit – who lived under both the brutalities of an apartheid legal system and the promises of a new constitutional democracy of South Africa – reflects powerfully on how such basic constitutional laws can foster moral formation and reformation. Smit writes:

> Morality changes, and very often it changes as a result of legal changes. Experience amply shows that forms of racism, sexism, homophobia, prejudice and discrimination, disregard for human dignity, violations of human rights, slavery, abuse, and in fact many practices of corruption, nepotism and exclusion often first have to be prohibited by law, before a major part of the population will change their minds to ac-

---

[111] See Frank Brennan, "An Australian Case Study on Law and Values", in *Law and Character*, 127–40.

[112] James E. Fleming, "Are Constitutional Courts Civic Educative Institutions? If So, What Do They Teach?", in *Law and Character*, 95–108.

[113] See further examples in John Witte, Jr., *The Blessings of Liberty: Human Rights and Religious Freedom in the Western Legal Tradition* (Cambridge: Cambridge University Press, 2019).

[114] Linda C. McClain, "Bigotry, Civility, and Reinvigorating Civic Education", in *Law and Character*, 109–26.

[115] Allen Calhoun, "'The True Freedom of the Christian Spirit': Martin Luther's Vision of Redistributive Taxation", in *Law and Character*, 177–92.

cept and share these convictions. In this sense, living in a city with just laws is indeed an important form of moral formation – as the Greek philosopher [Xenophilos] already taught.[116]

Fourth, modern constitutionalism altogether has moral qualities and analogies that Robert Bellah once called a nation's "civil religion"[117] – a form of public religion that undergirds and supports more particular and powerful forms of spiritual religion and morality. American constitutionalism is a good example.[118] The text of the United States Constitution is viewed as a quasi-sacred national document, secured in a national shrine, celebrated in national holidays and exhibitions, and confirmed in solemn oaths and pledges of allegiance. The text of the Constitution is authoritative in itself, a canon whose exact meaning remains the subject of endless debate and development. The writings of the founding fathers who created and ratified this document are also authoritative – like Hebrew prophets expounding the Torah, epistles glossing the gospels. The judges who interpret the Constitution are secular priests, who, after enduring long passages of ordination and confirmation, utter solemn public oaths to uphold the Constitution. Like priests standing at their high pulpits expounding the biblical commandment to "love thy neighbor as thyself", judges sit on their raised benches expounding the constitutional commandment to give "due process" and "equal protection" to all. Like congregants in the church, citizens of the state study these priestly interpretations of their authoritative text, debating their veracity, their utility, their allegiance to the original and evolving meaning of the canon.

This process and practice of state constitutionalism can, of course, easily become dangerous, even idolatrous. But it can also be a complement, even stepping stone, to a more robust spiritualism. Just as fairly administered state criminal laws not to kill or steal or bear false witness can anticipate and facilitate a

---

[116] Dirk J. Smit, "What abou' the lô? Adam Small on Law and Morality", in Robert Vosloo, ed., *Remembering Theologians – Doing Theology: Collected Essays 5* (Stellenbosch: Sun Press, 2013), 402–03, quoted and discussed in Robert Vosloo, "Law, Conscience, and Character Formation: A South African Case Study in Ricoeurian Perspectives", in *Law and Character*, 249–63, at 254.

[117] See, Robert N. Bellah and Phillip E. Hammond, *Varieties of Civil Religion* (San Francisco: Harper & Row, 1980). See also Philip E. Gorski, *American Covenant: A History of Civil Religion from the Puritans to the Present* (Princeton: Princeton University Press, 2019); Sanford Levinson, *Constitutional Faith* (Princeton: Princeton University Press, 1988).

[118] This paragraph is drawn from John Witte, Jr., "Law, Religion, and Metaphor", in *Risiko und Vertrauen / Risk and Trust: Festschrift für Michael Welker zum 70. Geburtstag*, ed. Günter Thomas and Heike Springhart (Leipzig: Evangelische Verlagsanhalt, 2017), 177–95, at 191.

deeper moral ethic of love, charity, and respect for one's neighbors, so a properly bounded state constitutional system of rules and rituals can conduce to a deeper appreciation for the scripture, canons, and practices of chosen faith traditions.[119]

Fifth, a good number of modern rights laws enable citizens to exercise their moral agency and responsibilities and induce their fellow citizens to exercise theirs.[120] Anabaptist theologian Stanley Hauerwas is right to warn that human rights norms today can become a grammar of greed and grasping, of self-promotion and self-aggrandizement at the cost of one's neighbor and one's relationship to God.[121] But Christians from the start have claimed their rights and freedoms first and foremost in order to discharge the moral duties of the faith. Claiming one's right to worship God, to avoid false gods, to observe the Sabbath, and to use God's name properly enables one to discharge the duties of love owed to God under the First Table of the Decalogue. Claiming one's rights to life, property, and reputation, or to the integrity of one's marriage, family, and household gives one's neighbor the chance to honor the duties of love in the Second Table of the Decalogue – to not murder, steal, or bear false witness; to not dishonor parents or breach marital vows; to not covet, threaten, or violate "anything that is your neighbor's."[122] To insist on these Second Table rights can also be an act of love toward your neighbors, giving them the opportunity and accountability necessary to learn and discharge their moral duties.

Viewed this way, many rights claims are not selfish grasping at all – even if they happen to serve one's own interests. Rights claims can reflect and embody love of God and neighbor. The claims of the poor and needy, the widow and the orphan, the child and the stranger, and the "least" of society are, in part, invitations for others to serve God and neighbor: "As you did it to one of the least of these … you did it to me", Jesus said.[123] To insist on the rights of self-defense and the protection and integrity of one's body or of loved ones, or to bring private claims and support public prosecution of those who rape, batter, starve, abuse, torture, or kidnap you or your loved ones is, in part, an invitation for others to

---

[119] This is an extension of the Protestant "uses of the law" framework, which contrasts the civil use of the law that conduces to civil morality and the pedagogical use of the law that conduces to spiritual righteousness. See discussion in John Witte, Jr., "The Uses of Law for the Formation of Character: A Classic Protestant Doctrine for Late-Modern Liberal Societies?" in *Religion and Character*, 261–83.

[120] The next two paragraphs are distilled from Witte, *The Blessings of Liberty*, 290–303.

[121] Stanley Hauerwas, *The Hauerwas Reader* (Durham, NC: Duke University Press, 2009), chaps. 4, 6, 7, 8, 9, 11, 12, 16, 21, 22, 26, 28, 31 with summary in id., "How to Think Theologically about Rights", *Journal of Law and Religion* 30 (2015): 402–13.

[122] Exodus 20:17.

[123] Matthew 25:40.

respect the divine image and "temple of the Lord" that each person embodies.[124] To insist on the right to education and training, and the right to work and earn a fair wage is, in part, an invitation for others to respect God's call to each of us to prepare for and pursue our distinct vocation.[125] To sue for contractual performance, to claim a rightful inheritance, to collect on a debt or insurance claim, to bring an action for discrimination or wrongful discharge from a job serves, in part, to help others to live out the Golden Rule – to do unto others as you would have them do unto you.[126] To petition the government for due process and equal protection; to seek compensation for unjust taxes or unlawful takings or searches of property; or to protest governmental abuse, deprivation, persecution, or violence – all of these are, in part, calls for political officers to live up to the lofty ideals of justice that the Bible ascribes to the political office. To sue for freedoms of speech and press or for the right to vote is, in part, a call for others to respect God's generous calling for each of us to serve as a prophet, priest, and sovereign on this earth. And to insist on freedom of conscience and free exercise of religion is to force others to respect the prerogatives of God, whose loving relationship with his children cannot be trespassed upon by any person or institution.

Finally, the legal profession itself can be an exemplar of moral virtue. To be sure, Shakespeare's *Henry VI* famously proclaimed: "The first thing we do, let's kill all the lawyers",[127] echoing Martin Luther's statement that "jurists are bad Christians."[128] Lawyers have certainly done their share to earn such opprobrium for their belligerence and bombast, their obstructionism and delay tactics, their hair-splitting casuistry, their pretentious self-indulgence and cleverly cloaked theft from their clients. But for all the excesses of those greedy and grubby lawyers who betray us, the law is at heart a noble profession – a "democratic aristocracy", as Alexis de Tocqueville once put it, a "priesthood of civility", as Justice Thurgood Marshall later put it. Lawyers are essential officers of our courts – charged with the responsibility of maintaining our system of justice and equity, of vindicating the rights and liberties, privileges and immunities of our fellow citizens and subjects. Lawyers are essential trustees of our legal tradition – equipped for the task of carrying on the great experiment of fostering life, liberty, and the pursuit of happiness within a democratic society dedicated to the rule of law. And lawyers are essential leaders of public life – called both to dem-

---

[124] 1 Corinthians 3:16.
[125] Ephesians 4:1.
[126] Matthew 7:12.
[127] *Henry VI, Part 2*, IV, 2.
[128] *Martin Luthers Werke: Tischreden*, 6 vols. (Weimar: H. Böhlaus Nachfolger, 1912-), vol. 3, No. 2809b; see also ibid., vol. 6, Nos. 7029-30.

onstrate and to facilitate the noble virtues of charity and compassion, education and learning, forgiveness and peacemaking.

In late modern liberal societies, lawyers are required to be "paradigmatic liberal citizens", Australian jurist Reid Mortenson argues, seeking to advance their clients' interests through orderly and organized procedures that hew to a baseline of morality and conscionability, rather than through dangerous self-help and unethical self-promotion.[129] Lawyers are also called to discharge a morally responsible role in law and business, American legal ethics expert Robert Cochran continues. Litigators advocate for each side and enable judges and juries to make better decisions based on fuller knowledge of the facts and law. Business lawyers draft documents and negotiate deals enabling businesses to employ people and meet the needs of customers.[130] Such legal representation should employ and develop the virtues of truthfulness, courage, justice, and prudence. Yes, legal representation carries moral risks for both lawyers and clients. Constant advocacy for clients may cause a lawyer to become argumentative and less forthcoming in areas of life where these qualities are not justified. Some lawyers encourage clients to act in unnecessarily self-serving ways, reinforcing the selfish instincts of clients. But the better role for the lawyer is that of a "friend" in the classical sense, Cochran argues, initiating moral discourse between the lawyer and the client and encouraging moral growth for both of them.[131]

These and other examples illustrate that modern state law does and can – in discrete and circumscribed ways – still foster character formation, ethical education, and communication of values in the late modern pluralistic societies. State laws and moral norms interact somewhat – as in a Venn diagram – though they do not overlap entirely. State laws have many other sources and goals beyond morality, and moral norms have many other forms and forums for their implementation beyond those of the state. Thus the state and its laws help to cultivate private and public morality, but they can do only so much in the moral field. Late modern societies also need broader communities and narratives to stabilize, deepen, and exemplify the natural inclinations and rational norms of responsibility, sociability, and morality that all human beings have written on their hearts, if not embedded in their genes. Even the most progressive liberal societies need models and exemplars of love and fidelity, trust and

---

[129] Reid Mortenson, "The Clergy of Liberalism: Lawyers' Character, Virtue, and Moral Education in Pluralized Societies", in *Law and Character*, 215–32.

[130] See further Thomas Pfeiffer, "The Law of Contracts and Ethics: Interrelation in Spite of Separation", in *Law and Character*, 165–76; E. Allan Farnsworth, "Parables about Promises: Religious Ethics and Contract Enforceability", in *Law and Character*, 151–64.

[131] Robert F. Cochran, Jr., "Legal Representation and the Character Formation of Lawyers and Clients", in *Law and Character*, 233–48.

sacrifice, commitment and community to give these inborn natural teachings further content and coherence. They need the help of stable institutions beyond the state – families, neighborhoods, churches, schools, charities, hospitals, recreational, athletic, artistic, and creative associations, and much more – to form the rich moral characters and refined ethical outlooks of their citizens, to teach both the minimal morality of duty that keeps the sinners within all of us at bay and the morality of aspiration that brings out the angels in all of us who are devoted to love of God, neighbor, and self.

Chapter 5

Health Care

The institutions of health care and medicine today are prime sites for character development, ethical education, and communication of values in late modern pluralistic societies. Medicine, together with rapid scientific and medical technological development, serves to relieve "pain and disturbance of peace of mind" and thus corresponds to the great visions of true happiness suggested by the Greek philosopher Epicurus (341–271/270 BC). Health care serves to protect the suffering and the weak, offering help and comfort not only to those affected by illness but also to their relatives and friends. It therefore meets the highest standards of a humanitarian ethos.

The institutions and professionals of modern health care are deeply interwoven with other prominent social spheres and systems in late modern societies that we address in this volume. Health care professionals provide care, education, and nurture for all family members – in sickness and in health, from birth to death. Pastors, chaplains, deacons, and others provide vital spiritual services to those in hospitals and suffering from sickness and injury and family members. State officials provide vast resources for health care research and services and operate many public hospitals alongside private hospitals and health services. Complex laws and procedures regulate the health care and pharmaceutical industries; licenses and patents facilitate and protect scientific research and medical advances; state courts try cases of medical malpractice, medical fraud, and financial and bodily abuse. Many public and private academic research facilities and laboratories, together with large university departments and professional schools, provide vital medical training, scientific experimentation, and technological and pharmaceutical developments designed to expand and improve health care. Health care is a massive economic market, comprising some eight to ten percent of the GDP of most late modern pluralistic nations, 15 to 18 percent in the United States. Communication about health, medicine, and treatment options is now also a massive industry in print and online. And the military in most late modern pluralistic nations maintains its own health care system, catering to the distinct medical needs and injuries, often tragic, faced by military personnel. Since professional health care is such a nexus of services and relationships in late modern pluralistic societies, it can lay claim to the top position in terms of ethos and charisma.

Our interdisciplinary research team – comprising specialists in medicine, medical ethics, psychology, theology, and health care – has uncovered several common challenges that this formidable and rapidly changing social sphere faces in late modern pluralistic societies and the impact of these challenges on character formation, ethical education, and the communication of values. We offer a sampling of their findings here.[132]

Costs versus Care

The tensions between a physician's duty of care to each patient and the costs of ever-improving medical care cause many of the problems of health care in liberal democratic societies today. German medical ethicist Eva Winkler has examined the constantly increasing cost pressure on doctors today, especially in the clinical care of the population.[133] How can the quality of medical treatment and trust in the medical profession be maintained, Winkler asks, if economic and political warnings against overly expensive interventions and therapies constantly accompany the work? How should doctors react to medically promising but highly costly developments in the pharmaceutical industry and medical technology? Can and should they try to prevent the economic profit interests of investors from deforming an essentially egalitarian health-care system in a class-based society?

Winker argues that the obligation to provide optimal medical care for each individual patient must be part and product of an integrated organizational ethic that balances the costs of a highly functioning medical system with costs of a range of other services that cater to health, safety, and welfare as well as justice, peacemaking, and human flourishing. But in a day of rising costs and taxes, and increasing political and ideological divides over what is essential, this balancing act is often a daunting ordeal. The improvement of a mul-

---

[132] Michael Welker, Eva Winkler, John Witte, Jr., and Stephen Pickard, eds., *The Impact of Health Care on Character Formation, Ethical Education, and the Communication of Values in Late Modern Pluralistic Societies* (Leipzig: Evangelische Verlagsanstalt, 2023) [hereafter *Health Care and Character*].

[133] Eva C. Winkler, "Time for a New Oath? The Role of the Individual Physician's Ethos and Institutional Ethics in the Face of Economization of the Health-Care System", in *Health Care and Character,* 23–33.

tisystemic orientation for a society-wide ethos must therefore be brought to bear on medicine and health care as well as on other spheres of activity.

Anthony D. Ho, a highly respected international cancer and stem cell researcher, uses four case studies to shed light on the dramatic problems inherent in the modern health-care system.[134] He tells of a very wealthy and strong-willed CEO who, after several unsuccessful attempts at chemotherapy, took a private flight to a meeting of the twelve top cancer researchers in New Orleans in 1984/85. Only one of them advised him against any further attempts at therapy. He decided to follow the majority opinion – that is, the advice to have a stem cell transplant–but died before treatment could begin. Ho comments soberly:

1. Most experts have a propensity to come up with the "smartest" proposals in the name of medical advances, especially in a conference of professionals ... This raises the ethical question of how far a patient with terminal disease should be encouraged to undergo another experimental treatment with unknown risks.
2. Very few medical experts–in this case only one–have the courage to provide realistic advice when confronted with a dying patient, especially one with adequate financial resources. This raises the question of character formation required for proper interaction with patients.
3. Some studies have shown that in every health care system in the "developed" world, a disproportionately large amount of health-care resources is spent on attempts to prolong life of patients who are terminally ill ... This raises the ethical question of proportionality and of what constitutes the appropriate allocation of resources.
4. In the everyday clinical environment, resources go beyond the availability of funds. They include human resources ... Can the extensive demand of resources be justified when the intensive care of one terminally ill patient effectively reduces the manpower and time needed for care of other patients?[135]

Ho also recounts one of the first successful stem cell therapies in San Diego, in 1992, the $350,000 cost of which prompted a reporter to ask, shockingly at the time, whether this use of vast resources that could have saved numerous lives was justified. He concludes his study with an encouraging report on the development of the initially highly emotionalized debate on stem cell research in the United States since 1960, and then shows how, in Germany, a comprehensive process of investigation and understanding among civil, political, scientific, legal, and religious authorities could lead to a fruitful exemplary model for ethical decision-making in society.

German theologian and ethicist Günter Thomas shows how care of the sick and injured was, for centuries, a highly individualized form of care, based on

---

[134] Anthony D. Ho, "The Impact of Advances in Stem Cell and Genome Research on Ethical Decision-Making", in *Health Care and Character*, 65–75.
[135] Ibid., 54–55.

person-to-person relationships.[136] Today, by contrast, medicine and health care are much more highly institutionalized, involving not just hospitals, clinics, and other professional medical institutions but also insurance systems, public and political health-care bureaucracies, sundry ethical oversight committees of doctors and nursing staff, and the very different expectations of patients and their relatives. How can this complex network of different value systems, orientations, and expectations be brought into view in a meaningful way? Thomas calls for organized communities of solidarity, which must always be both inclusive and exclusive in order to function at all. He asserts that religious, scientific, and civil contexts must be discussed in relation to broader ideas of a good, fulfilled, and successful life, without jeopardizing the protection of the weakest and most vulnerable, but also without jeopardizing the preservation of organized health care. This delicate balance requires intensive collaboration between those who hold religiously and ethically based values and those who face ethical and practical challenges in health care in order to counter a loss of orientation, inflation of expectations, and the associated burnout.

Geriatric psychiatrist Christine Thomas focuses these challenges on the medical treatment of elderly and frail patients.[137] She describes conflicts over protecting patients' sovereignty and autonomy in the interpretation of their will while dealing with their decision-making options. Such conflicts often arise between patients and their relatives (usually of the younger generations), or between patients and their families, on one hand, and medical and therapeutic practitioners and caregivers, on the other. A wide spectrum of problems arises, ranging from unrealistic demands for maximum and expensive therapy to what she calls a resigned "nihilism" on the part of people who are terminally ill – that is, a resigned or even apathetic attitude, not only in those directly affected by the suffering but in their relatives as well. The limits of hospital funding and the limits of the mental and physical capacities of medical and nursing staff are also significant. As a minimum solution, Thomas sees the indispensable ethical requirement of responsible treatment of the elderly and infirm as requiring (1) the affirmation of a community of solidarity, (2) the principle of doing no harm in medical care, (3) the firm will to evaluate and choose wisely between overmedication and underuse of therapeutic and nursing resources, and (4) personal communication between nursing staff and patients and ethical counseling or mediation in the event of conflict.

Thorsten Moos, a theological ethicist and medical ethicist with experience in hospital chaplaincy, explains why hospital chaplaincy has experienced

---

[136] Günter Thomas, "Mercy under Conditions of Scarcity and the Need for Organization", in *Health Care and Character*, 35–44.

[137] Christine Thomas, "Ethical Tensions in the Medical Treatment of Elderly Patients in Geriatrics and Geriatric Psychiatry", in *Health Care and Character*, 45–52.

very intensive development and recognition in recent years.[138] These chaplaincies must concern themselves not only with respecting the autonomy of the sick person (an autonomy emphasized by many members of our research team) but also with the mental, psychological, and therapeutic limits and borderline questions about the "free will" of a patient in a life-threatening situation. The intensification of professional medical ethics toward decision-making techniques in difficult treatment situations has led to a new appreciation and new educational programs for clinical pastoral care. This development has fostered a new openness to including clinical pastoral care in the broad field of interactions among doctors, patients, relatives and neighbors, the clinical nursing staff, and various advisory voices.

Moos emphasizes that this enhanced level of competence and participation is required to deal carefully with different ethical perspectives and convictions, not only among patients but also among clinical staff. The new challenges of hospital chaplaincy, he says, require more than adding skills to the set of old pastoral skills. Above all, it requires giving attention to the difficult but highly valuable ethical goal of giving the sick person a voice in any discussions between the treating and caring professionals, on one hand, and, on the other hand, the voices of relatives and friends on the other – especially in situations of deep personal conflict and those when patients have difficulty articulating their own will.

Hard Ethical Decisions and Trade-offs in Health Care

The enormous increase in diagnostic, therapeutic, and technology-supported surgical possibilities, particularly in neurosurgery and genetic technology, over the past two decades requires physicians not only to deal with explosive cost increases but also to make difficult trade-offs regarding the patient's gain in quality of life through an intervention. Neurosurgeons Andreas Unterberg and Pavlina Lenga address this problem.[139] They argue from professional experience that complex pathologies, such as brain tumors and spinal cord tumors, require not only sophisticated surgical and clinical capabilities but also highly ethical trade-offs between the exhaustion of medical and surgical options and the responsible perspective on patient welfare after risky medical interventions. Unterberg and Lenga highlight the need for candid and comprehensive

---

[138] Thorsten Moos, "Health-Care Chaplains and Medical Ethics: Clinical and Educational Experiences", in *Health Care and Character*, 165–74.

[139] Andreas Unterberg and Pavlina Lenga, "The Impact of Advances in Surgical Techniques and Quality-of-Life Considerations on Ethical Decision-Making and Education in Neurosurgery", in *Health Care and Character*, 101–17.

communication between the attending physicians and the patient as well as with the trainees, including discussion of the growing range of surgical options and their benefits and risks. The authors discuss the difficulties of measuring quality of life, particularly in the presence of complex pathologies, and they identify fields that require indispensable consultation in larger and multidisciplinary collegial circles.

Other authors similarly illustrate the great complexity of medical assessment and decision-making processes in difficult life situations and social controversies. German medical ethicists Karla Alex and Eva Winkler draw attention to genetics, genome editing, and epigenetics, which are at the center of recent popular scientific and ethical discussions, often driven by scientifically controversial opinions and moral convictions.[140] They deal with common erroneous views, such as those that humans are completely determined by their genetic constitution (genetic essentialism) or that their development is strongly determined by their genes (strong genetic determinism). They raise awareness of the many ethical dangers of these views, from misjudgments about individual responsibility to inadequate pregnancy counseling and perspectives on challenges in future population development.

American physician Ruth M. Farrell, who focuses on women's health, shows that the complexity of genetic information and the burden of uncertainty in dealing with it before birth are very challenging for patients, families, and society.[141] Genetic information not only is potentially emotionally stressful but also has far-reaching consequences for life choices, including the decision whether to terminate a pregnancy. Farrell emphasizes how important medical-ethical counseling is in the run-up to such a decision. Weighing the values, needs, and goals of women seeking advice (as well as their families), and tapping into the potential therapeutic and social support available to those affected is of great importance. The social and moral value systems that can influence personal and ethical decisions in a helpful or problematic way must also be taken into account.

These decision-making situations are further complicated by advances in genetic newborn screening, which medical psychologist Beate Ditzen and geneticist Christian P. Schaaf examine closely.[142] These diagnostic tools can identify specific diseases in newborns that require early intervention to avert health

---

[140] Karla Alex and Eva C. Winkler, "Ethical Discourse on Epigenetics and Genome Editing: The Risk of [Epi-] Genetic Determinism and Scientifically Basic Assumptions", in *Health Care and Character*, 77–99.

[141] Ruth M. Farrell, "The Acceptance of Genetic Technologies by Individuals, Societies, and Health-Care Systems", in *Health Care and Character*, 65–75.

[142] Beate Ditzen and Christian P. Schaaf, "Family Decision-Making in Times of Genomic Newborn Screening", in *Health Care and Character*, 137–49.

risks or hazards. Such interventions require comprehensive consultations, not only with regard to the diagnostic possibilities but also with regard to possible imponderables and uncertainties in the prognoses. The authors recommend a scale with five points of view for possible decisions, giving particular importance to counseling that takes account of family medical histories. However, they also present a series of typical reactions from individuals and families as well as advice in situations of subjective and objective uncertainties about the outcome of a decision.

The ethics of digitalization in medicine, care, health care, and prenatal and reproductive medicine is an important factor in many medical-ethical issues today. Medical ethicists Giovanni Rubeis and Nadia Primc examine this topic.[143] They begin by addressing several common prejudices and generalized fears about the development opportunities in this area and formulate three criteria for perspectives on positive developments: (1) emphasizing the high relevance of patients' autonomy, their active participation in the treatment process, and the critical examination of possible factors that impair or prevent this empowerment; (2) distinguishing technologies that support patient autonomy from those that pose risks to patient well-being; and (3) examining the consequences of introducing nonhuman actors into clinical care processes, and whether they enhance or minimize patients' willingness to trust clinical staff.

The Challenges of Nursing

Medical ethicist Karen Nolte describes a highly significant problem in the entire health-care system, namely the often chronic shortage of qualified nurses.[144] The dramatic nature of the problem became apparent on a broad scale during the COVID-19 pandemic, when the resources of the medical and therapeutic care system could not be adequately utilized due to a shortage of qualified nurses and the overburdening and burnout of the nurses that were in place. Nolte identifies major deficits and problems in the education, compensation, and organization of medical nursing, even as she writes with appreciation of the great financial and institutional achievements of the profession. She suggests reforms to improve training and career opportunities, which have long received insufficient attention.

Nolte looks at the development of nursing in Germany since 1782, a time when nursing was strongly supported by religious and moral foundations,

---

[143] Giovanni Rubeis and Nadia Primc, "Ethical Aspects of Digital Transformation in Medicine and Health Care", in *Health Care and Character*, 121–36.

[144] Karen Nolte, "On the History of Nursing Ethos in Germany", in *Health Care and Character*, 153–63.

and nurses usually organized in sisterhoods associated with Christian denominations. Nurses then were expected to tend not only to the physical and material needs of their patients but also to their mental and spiritual needs. Today this nursing ethic is perceived as exploitative and oppressive. Modern health care has greatly reduced the religious dimensions of nursing, and strongly emphasized medical care instead. The leadership roles of head nurses were already strengthened at a time when many German authors were still propagating subordination of nurses to the authority of doctors. Then, in the postwar period, as fewer and fewer young women were willing to "sacrifice" a private life and family in favor of working in health care, Germany began to recruit nurses first in southern European countries, later in Asia, and finally in Latin America. The extent of the crisis in the nursing system became apparent when the political authorities no longer felt able to bear the costs of nursing care in hospitals and rehabilitation facilities, while at the same time nurses called for increased professional recognition and better financial resources.

Health Care in Interdisciplinary Perspective

Health care is not just about science and surgery, the body and medicine, hospitals and health care institutions. Health care is also interwoven with many other social institutions and spheres of life, and thus requires analysis from many other disciplines. We offer a couple of examples here.

German theologian Gregor Etzelmüller concentrates on the human question of health and healing beyond the capabilities of medical and therapeutic forces.[145] He follows the insights and impulses of Viktor von Weizsäcker, one of the founders of psychosomatic medicine, that people in need of healing also ask about "the destiny of their lives." In doing so, they generally underestimate the wisdom of their body, which in many illnesses demands a reorientation of their lives. In developing a holistic ethic of health care, Etzelmüller draws on several brilliant philosophical and interdisciplinary voices of the twentieth century (Whitehead, Heidegger, Arendt, and Nussbaum), who shed light on the complex psychosomatic and psychosocial constitution of human existence. He also draws on the comprehensive anthropology of the Apostle Paul, which focused on the integration of the "flesh, body, heart, soul, conscience, and spirit" of each person, and the need for individual and social orientation toward the powers of the spirit. Etzelmüller argues that the legally and ethically relevant search for justice and protection of the weak-as well as the striving for the comprehensive spiritual gifts of faith, love, and hope - must be part of com-

---

[145] Gregor Etzelmüller, "Medical Anthropology and Theology on Human Destiny", in *Health Care and Character*, 175-95.

prehensive health care. Without losing sight of the concrete medical needs of the patient's body, the comprehensive ethical, mental, and spiritual dimensions of human life should be kept present in all reflections on health and healing.

Clinical psychologist Peter Kirsch concretizes this view in offering psychotherapeutic perspectives on so-called personality disorders.[146] He emphasizes the need for health-care professionals to attend to personal orientation and control, gaining pleasure and avoiding displeasure, gaining and consolidating connectedness and self-esteem. In all these situations of need, Kirsch argues, psychotherapy should help people to identify their elementary needs, values, and goals for action. In doing so, psychotherapists must avoid all tendencies toward professional paternalism and must absolutely respect the autonomy and self-determination of patients. Psychotherapy reaches its limits when the goals of those seeking help come into conflict with fundamental values of society or the therapist.

Concluding Reflections

The studies summarized in this chapter point to the great scientific and medical technological developments of recent years and the increasingly efficient performance of doctors and therapists. These health-care professionals have consolidated the outstanding reputation of medicine and health care within the network of social systems. However, the inflation of costs associated with these positive developments and the inflation of expectations associated with medical performance are increasing the social, political, and economic pressure on those working in medicine and health care, leading to personal impairments, wear and tear on bodies and spirits, and burnout. Doctors and nurses face major challenges in being faithful to the medical and nursing ethos. Many areas of society are seeing a neglect of the financial and appreciation of the people who support the system. Future studies on character development and ethical education will need to confront unrealistic ideas of quality of life and the unbounded personal freedom of patients as well as better self-care for medical professionals.

---

[146] Peter Kirsch, "Psychotherapy, Personality, and the Role of Values", in *Health Care and Character*, 197–202.

Chapter 6

Academic Research

Ethics and Research Universities

In many countries, academic research is closely associated with universities and their combination of research and teaching. It therefore makes sense to begin this chapter by reflecting on "The Idea of a Research University",[147] where the term "research" is understood to mean both research and teaching. However, this perspective, which is reflected in the international rankings, ignores the fact that universities are not the only places where significant scientific research is carried out.

One example of research beyond the university can be found in Germany, where cutting-edge research is conducted to some extent at influential nonacademic institutions with high levels of state funding. These institutions include the research centers of the Max Planck Society, the Helmholtz Association of German Research Centers, the Fraunhofer Society, and the German Cancer Research Center. It is true that most of these institutions are closely linked to universities. They are involved in university teaching and research by providing teaching staff, designing degree courses, and running joint graduate colleges. However, their research successes are attributed to the institutions and not to the associated universities, a fact that unfortunately has a negative impact on the position of German universities in international rankings. In many countries, too, great scientific achievements are also made by the research departments of large corporations.

---

[147] See William Schweiker, "The Idea of a Research University", in William Schweiker, Michael Welker, John Witte, Jr., and Stephen Pickard, eds., *The Impact of Academic Research on Character Formation, Ethical Education, and the Communication of Values in Late Modern Pluralistic Societies* (Leipzig: Evangelische Verlagsanstalt; Eugene, OR: Wipf & Stock, 2021) [hereafter *Academic Research and Character*], 23–38.

The combination of research and teaching found in universities and beyond is a valuable asset to a society interested in character development. The active participation of students from different countries and different academic disciplines is particularly beneficial. A global intellectual community that is committed to the concentrated search for knowledge and truth and that has developed many forms of critical examination of all truth claims is an excellent medium for character development, ethical education, and communication of values in all societies of the world. However, the breadth of international and multidisciplinary communication found in universities also entails dangers. In addition to the disciplinarily controlled scientific search for truth, ethical concerns can arise that reinforce political and moral expectations or bring conflicts that are far removed from science into university communication processes. The National Socialist contamination of German universities after 1933 provides a particularly frightening example of this kind of ideological undermining of the academy. Likewise, the history of slavery and the toleration of racism at renowned research universities in the United States right into the twentieth century. Even today, extreme political and military conflicts can have devastating effects on the intellectual climate, even at highly respected research universities (for example, currently at Harvard).

American ethicist William Schweiker begins the exploration of our research team on the impact of academic research on character formation by first briefly discussing the historical motives behind the founding of universities.[148] He sees a leitmotif in the connection between the question of knowledge in the world of facts and knowledge in matters of lifestyle. The founders of the first universities – initially in Bologna in 1088 – assumed an ordered universe of knowledge that needed to be explored and developed with knowledge (*scientia*) and wisdom (*sapientia*). They saw the natural universe as being connected to a religious universe. An ultimately religious cosmology led to theology being placed at the top of the academic disciplines, followed by law and medicine.

According to Schweiker, the modern university has moved a long way away from its founding ideas of a religious or moral horizon of inquiry, the concept of the unity of human reason, and belief in the possibility of character formation through scientific training. He describes today's university as a collection of different disciplines with their own methods, purposes, and scientific norm, whose differences lead to "intellectual silos" that largely have to forgo communication with other silos. This compartmentalization is accompanied by deficiencies in intellectual orientation and by early professionalization.[149] The situation is exacerbated by the fact that research and teaching are driven by economic needs

---

[148] Ibid.
[149] Ibid., 26.

and career interests, and are supported by technological, medical, military, athletic, and political background interests.

Schweiker offers a brief overview of the major philosophical and cultural-scientific developments of the last centuries, from the ideal of value-neutral investigation to the concentration on scientific methods, the replacement of bipolar approaches by multimodal ones, the organization of interdisciplinary research processes focused on significant topics, and the conviction that all researchers are not merely observers but are practical actors in their contributions to scientific development.[150] All of these circumstances lead to concrete ethical consequences for life at research universities today. Researchers must develop a sense of responsibility for their own contributions to the advancement of knowledge. This responsibility is a social responsibility with regard to fellow teachers and fellow students and ultimately with regard to the entire university and its value systems, not only in the search for truth but also in the pursuit of justice, freedom, philanthropy, and ecological prudence. Schweiker puts it in a nutshell: "Enhancement of the Integrity of Life."[151] The university must understand itself not only as an intellectual community of truth-seekers but also as a morally communicating community that cultivates the reciprocal gift or withdrawal of esteem and respect for researchers and scholars as well as their associated development of self-respect.[152]

American sociologist Andreas Glaeser's contribution follows on from this.[153] Glaeser uses a broad concept of "institution", which he defines as "any stable social arrangement that is formed and maintained by human beings."[154] The control of all institutionalizations is assigned to ethics, which can take many different forms. All self-confident and stable human communities develop ethics, he writes. Glaeser examines the characteristic processes by which social life unfolds. These processes and their ethical control then shape individual personalities and their character formation. Of course, personal validation is central to these developmental processes, but all validations are characterized by a continuous flow of recognition, affirmations, and resonances. (One must also add by experiences of withdrawal of recognition, denial of affirmations, and loss of resonance.)

---

[150] Ibid., referencing Stephen Toulmin, *The Return to Cosmology: Postmodern Science and the Theology of Nature* (Berkeley: University of California Press, 1982), 255–56.

[151] Ibid., 37 ff.

[152] William Schweiker has repeatedly drawn our attention to the great importance of developing self-esteem in moral communication processes.

[153] Andreas Glaeser, "Analyzing Actually Existing Ethics: A Hermeneutic-Institutionalist Approach", in *Academic Research and Character*, 39–63.

[154] Ibid., 39.

However, the ethical processes that shape individuals depend not only on communicative processes and resonant relationships but also on changes in broader institutional conditions and ecological frameworks. It is not only deliberate, targeted, or indifference- and negligence-induced processes of concealment that pose a serious problem, but also the reality that many actions and developments that would in fact be effectively beneficial for society cannot be achieved with available knowledge. Glaeser emphasizes the often-drastic changes in ideas and practices of freedom, both the negative freedom of resistance and denial as well as the positive freedom of affirmation and promotion of alternative developments. The plurality of "spheres of social life" in modernity, emphasized by sociological classics such as those of Georg Simmel and Max Weber, has enormously intensified and accelerated this development of the variants of freedom. It is important to recognize and acknowledge different scales and calibers of freedom and a constant process of review and evaluation that requires ethics and politics to work together. For this evaluation cannot be left to responsible individuals alone. Glaeser formulates the decisive challenge as follows: "What forms of institutions should we develop so that we can live valuable lives? In short: What are good institutions?"[155] Classical references to transcendental values are no more helpful here than naturalistic scientism or a well-intentioned romanticism of nature. Glaeser thus refers to the range of tasks undertaken by this series of consultations and publications regarding the development of character in late modern pluralistic societies.

The next three contributions from our research team examine the performance of scientific research in the face of the challenges just outlined. German mathematician Bernold Fiedler emphasizes the warning against metaphysical searches for orientation, but also against appealing to pure logic or pure faith as the last bastions of an "absolute truth."[156] He examines the power of correspondence theories and coherence theories of truth with special attention to mathematical approaches. He asks: What is the basis of the fundamental belief of all mathematicians in the consistency and coherence of mathematics, the trust in the coherence and consistency of nature in the natural sciences? He quotes at length the skeptical voice of Friedrich Nietzsche, that "it is still a metaphysical faith, on which our faith in Science is based – that we also, the knowing, the godless, and antimetaphysical, still take our fire from the conflagration which a millennia-old faith has kindled, that Christian faith, which was the faith of Plato as well, that God is truth, that truth is divine" – what Nietzsche calls a "great lie."[157] Fiedler acknowledges Karl Popper's position: "It is not the posses-

---

[155] Ibid., 62.

[156] Bernold Fiedler, "Absolute Truth – A Toxic Chimera?", in *Academic Research and Character*, 65–87.

[157] Ibid., 85, quoting F. W. Nietzsche, *Die fröhliche Wissenschaft* (1882).

sion of knowledge, of incontrovertible truths, that makes the scientist, but the ruthless, ceaseless search for truth."[158] The countless successes of knowledge in the sciences and the life-enhancing fruits of scientists' work support the belief in progress and a hope that drives all research.

German philosopher Rüdiger Bittner, in his skeptical contribution, warns against hopes of gaining moral guidance from academic work.[159] He denies that academic research can function as a place where we learn how to live well and how to live fruitfully together. Academic research helps us with practical problems, but not with moral questions. Classical philosophical positions since antiquity have seen this differently, but according to Bittner, knowledge has lost its ethical significance, as David Hume had already clearly recognized in his 1739 classic *A Treatise of Human Nature.* Bittner is convinced that academic research today is a collection of activities by many people who are involved in a variety of studies, but who do not pursue a common goal. The idea that science is a "truth-seeking community" is merely wishful thinking. At best, one could say that different people pursue different truths, especially interesting truths. Even if they do not directly promote economic interests, they are in competition with each other in their various disciplines and research institutions. At least occasionally, some of them do speak out on larger social, political, and ethically relevant issues, but Bittner is convinced that they are hardly ever heard. He admits that scientific research – as well as other forms of human reflection and experience – can help us to find out what is sensible and right to do. However, it is about knowledge of the course of the world, knowledge of what is useful, not knowledge of what is good. Bittner finds it comforting that we do not need a moral compass at all, because we can live well together without agreeing on how we should live. Of course, we have to come to terms, and we occasionally need forms and institutions that guarantee the success of arrangements. However, he does not recognize in scientific research any potential for orientation in this respect.

In his contribution to this research team, one of us (Michael Welker) does not share this skepticism about academic research, although he also sees the ambivalences of moral communication in academic research.[160] It is true that

---

[158] Ibid., 86, quoting Karl Popper, *The Logic of Scientific Discovery* (New York: Basic Books, 1959).

[159] Rüdiger Bittner, "Can Academic Research Be a Moral Guide?", in *Academic Research and Character*, 89–97.

[160] Michael Welker, "Joy of Discovery – Respect for the Search for Truth – Honesty: The Blessings of a Global Network of Research Universities", in *Academic Research and Character*, 99–106. Welker explores the concept of the "multimodal spirit of truth" more extensively in his 2019–20 Gifford Lectures, published as *In God's Image: An Anthropology of the Spirit*, trans. Douglas W. Stott (Grand Rapids: Eerdmans, 2021).

we are confronted with trivial and nontrivial truths, not only in scientific research but also in many situations in life, that we take an interest in them, and, depending on the situation and profession, also ask and search for them in a concentrated manner. Welker suggests distinguishing between different calibers of truth-seeking and speaking of a multimodal "spirit of truth" overall. For many people, subjective certainty is a guiding star in the search for truth. In education and science, the fixation on subjective certainty is submitted to critical scrutiny. In moral issues, consensus is highly valued and consensus theories of truth are developed. But in science and education, the fleeting nature of consensus, long-established common errors, and seductive or even enforced social consensus are noted. More sophisticated forms of knowledge of truth than certainty and consensus are recommended and further developed under the regulations of consistency, coherence, and criteria of factual correctness, such as empirical and historical verifiability and rationality.

In these processes of development, universities and their disciplinary manifestations have a variety of orientation potentials that can correct, improve, and refine the individual experience of life and the world. The correction of individual experiences of the world and life, which also should occur scientifically and on a larger scale, is particularly important in situations of political and media manipulation and oppression. Referring to the Berlin philosopher Volker Gerhardt, Welker draws attention to the new ethical appreciation of truth and the common search for truth in view of the devastating rise of fake news – for example, in Donald Trump's election campaigns in the United States. The suppression of free media and the manipulation of legal systems in autocratic systems are also reasons to value the truth ethically. Welker sees a bulwark against efforts to suppress truth, freedom, and justice (including in larger social contexts) in a global network of research universities and research institutions committed to the search for truth and sensitive to falsification of reality – even if these diverse efforts cannot be called up with a simple voice and simple messages.

Character and Ethics at the Intersection of Disciplines

The second part of our research project offers reflections on the common theme from the perspective of specific subjects and disciplines: from the natural scientists Jörg Hüfner and Michael Kirschfink, the historian Gary S. Hauk, the lawyer John Witte, Jr., the theologians Andreas Schüle and Stefan Alkier, and the biologist and theologian Celia Deane-Drummond.

German Physicist Jörg Hüfner begins by emphasizing that his academic task was to teach physics to students and support them in their research, including through his own research.[161] He did not view contributing to their character development and ethical education as part of his professional obligation. This observation initially leads to the sober conclusion that ethics is not a relevant topic within physics. In Hüfner's opinion, however, there is a need for cooperation between the natural sciences and ethics because many scientific developments raise ethical questions. For example, some problematic economic transformations are triggered by scientific and technological innovations. Or people are confronted with unintended consequences of scientific discovery – for example, global warming caused by carbon dioxide emissions since the beginning of industrialization, or the evolution of the internet and the possibility of secret mass surveillance as a threat to human rights. There are also political, legal, and moral problems in dealing with so-called whistleblowers.

German immunologist Michael Kirschfink follows a similar line.[162] He emphasizes the enormous achievements in biomedical research over the past hundred years and the beneficial impact of these advances on many areas of human life, but also the continuing "health gaps" between wealthy and poor countries. He addresses numerous ethical challenges but also recognizes the problematic reality that some researchers view dealing with ethical issues as a hindrance to scientific progress. In these situations of tension, Kirschfink argues, international efforts to develop guidelines for procedures play an important role. Such efforts apply not only to phases following extreme crisis situations (for example, after 1945), but also to the ongoing observation and assessment of international scientific, social, and political developments. The guiding principle here is the development of measures that prevent scientific misconduct and promote integrity in research and publications. The increasing importance of social and interdisciplinary participation in scientific and humanitarian progress poses a further challenge, as this results in an educational mandate toward broader publics. And despite the priority given to scientific qualifications, students must also be challenged and trained in ethical judgment.

One historical and one legal contribution speak for the humanities. American university historian Gary S. Hauk begins by examining the two-hundred-year development of the United States from a slavery-justifying society to one that broadly affirms the values of liberal pluralist societies.[163] He uses the history of Emory University (located in the Southern state of Georgia), where he

---

[161] Jörg Hüfner, "The Impact of Science on Ethics", in *Academic Research and Character*, 109–17.

[162] Michael Kirschfink, "Ethical Considerations in Biomedical Research: Welcome Guidance or Unwanted Restrictions to Scientific Progress?", in *Academic Research and Character*, 119–30.

[163] Gary S. Hauk, "Academic Bondage and Social Transformation: The Case of American Universities and Slavery", in *Academic Research and Character*, 131–51.

worked as a senior officer for many years, as a field of investigation. The university's namesake, John Emory, was the scion of one of the largest slave-owning families in the state of Maryland. He himself owned slaves, and as a Methodist bishop he joined the circles that argued that abolishing slavery abruptly would have strong negative consequences on both emancipated slaves and the economy as a whole. Some antebellum Emory faculty members offered various exculpatory maneuvers in their publications and teaching for those who wanted to maintain slavery. For example, they accused politicians and factory owners in the North of applying double standards as they maintained "white slavery" with poorly paid mill workers, especially women. Southerners emphasized the blessing of Christianizing "heathen" slaves. Pseudoscientific bases for racist stereotypes were promoted even at northern universities and by supposed opponents of slaveholding. These views were to continue to have a disastrous effect on education and legal practice well into the twentieth century.

Not until 1962 did the first African American student enroll at Emory University. But by the 1990 s, major changes led to Emory having the highest percentage of African American students among the top twenty-five universities in the country. In 2005, Emory began a broad-based process involving more than two thousand students, faculty, administrators, and alumni to make the history of slavery, racism, and its impact on the American national psyche and its universities an ongoing project and program of research and transformation. Hauk concludes his contribution with cautious remarks regarding the power of historical and academic work for social, cultural, political, religious, and legal transformation.

One of us (John Witte) takes up this latter theme in his contribution.[164] He asks why research and teaching in the field of law and religion have gained such momentum in recent decades. This development was triggered in part by numerous social, cultural, political, religious, and legal transformations. It is a return to forms of science and education that were naturally established at universities for almost a millennium, but which experienced a dramatic collapse with the Enlightenment in the middle of the eighteenth century. The revival of interest in this area of study can be traced to a variety of political and other developments, including the fall of the Berlin Wall, the collapse of the Soviet Union, democratic movements in former colonial and authoritarian regimes in Africa and Latin America, and, more recently, signs of decay in liberal-democratic environments under the influence of both political and religious forces, civil society commitments to human rights and human dignity, and more. These developments have greatly stimulated international research on law and religion.

---

[164] John Witte, Jr., "The Educational Values of Studying Law and Religion", in *Academic Research and Character*, 153–68.

Witte names eight focal points of this research: first, issues of religious freedom and the relationship between politics and religion with regard to fundamental social institutions, such as the family, education, and welfare; second, the position and role of religion and religious freedom in the "pantheon of human rights"; third, the form and quality of the role of law within each of the major world religions; fourth, the contributions of the legal systems within religious institutions to the wider realm of secular politics and culture. Further focal points concern, fifth, the role of religion and law in the more recent transformations with regard to family and sexual ethics; sixth, confrontations with the truth claims of a worldview shaped by the natural sciences and classical positions of natural law; seventh, the interesting overlap between professional ethics among lawyers on one hand and clerics on the other; and, eighth, the question about the extent to which contemporary jurisprudence can absorb and use "religious and other comprehensive doctrines" in addition to scientific neutrality and extreme rationality.

The contributions by an Old Testament scholar and a New Testament scholar and the contribution by a biologist and theologian add decidedly religious and theological perspectives in academic contexts. German Old Testament scholar Andreas Schüle sees growing tensions between a dramatically increasing knowledge of the world in which we live and increasing difficulties in answering central questions of orientation in major processes of cultural change.[165] In contrast to the common prejudicial assumption that the ancient world has no helpful ethical insights to offer the contemporary world, he concentrates on two central biblical texts that examine the relationship between theology and the natural scientific understanding of the time in which they were written: the creation account in Genesis 1, and the theology of creation in Psalm 104. Schüle shows that both texts relate to God and God's creation in different ways, and that they react in different ways to ideological and philosophical impulses from their surroundings. By presenting conflicting claims to truth in creative dialogue, these texts reveal connections between the scientific and theological thinking of their time, which still provide useful food for thought today, especially in their imaginative and playful "interplay of scientific and theological ideas."[166]

German New Testament scholar Stefan Alkier considers the relationship between New Testament scholarship and practical theology, starting with extra-theological perspectives.[167] The acquisition of a spoken language and the skills of reading and text production shape the development of human identity, both

---

[165] Andreas Schüle, "Emergence of Truth", in *Academic Research and Character*, 169–77.
[166] Ibid., 178.
[167] Stefan Alkier, "Forming Identity by Scripture", in *Academic Research and Character*, 179–96.

individually and collectively. This development, however, is a process of interpretation that does not allow individuals and groups to gain a complete and self-contained view of themselves. They remain partially withdrawn from themselves. Nevertheless, language and textual culture lead to processes of fruitful self-opening which, in conjunction with theological impulses and content, help to shape and form identity individually and collectively. Alkier uses the so-called Sermon on the Mount as an example of this kind of identity formation, which would be misunderstood if the text were seen only as an instruction for a happy life (193). Rather, the verses of the Sermon on the Mount focus on a life greater than merely earthly human life – the life of the kingdom of God, which includes earthly life but goes far beyond it. The text opens our perception to a vision beyond the experience of finite life in flesh and blood, a perspective that includes but exceeds this earthly experience of finitude. By beatifying those who hunger for justice and seek peace, the text offers a view of a life that entrusts itself and its surroundings to the action of the divine spirit and its powers. This is anything but an indefinite openness to the future and a vague religious belief. It is a matter of justifiable knowledge and truth claims that have been proven over long periods of time, which can deal with empirical and historical falsifications without fail.

English biologist and theologian Celia Deane-Drummond offers an emphatically interdisciplinary contribution to the discussion of character formation and ethical education in academic research.[168] Like the skeptical and agnostic philosopher Rüdiger Bittner, she is centrally oriented toward Aristotle and the concept of prudence (*phronesis*). However, she is convinced that the development of prudence cannot be achieved without "practical wisdom" (*sofia*) and a connection between conscience (*synderesis*) and responsibility (*efthyni*). Deane-Drummond refers to the clearly expressed will among her science students to understand the value of their scientific work and to contribute to the common good and the beneficial impact of scientific work on society as a whole. She refers to the phenomenon of "troublesome knowledge", or the disorientation experienced by students making the transition from one familiar realm of study (say, science) to a new stage of learning and cognition (say, theology or the humanities generally).[169] Finally, she warns against retreating to "minimalist professional frameworks", not only in scientific work but also in ethical education. Rather, she encourages the fostering of imagination and conscience in the hope that research communities will nurture responsible research.[170]

---

[168] Celia Deane-Drummond, "Forming Research Scientists? Developing Practical Wisdom and Virtue in Multidisciplinary Academic Frameworks", in *Academic Research and Character*, 197–210.
[169] Ibid., 202.
[170] Ibid., 199.

Conclusions

The basic human need to know and to make sense of the context and times in which we live lies at the root of all academic research. The pursuit of knowledge inevitably entails principles, practices, and procedures that shape the missions of institutions and the values of the people who inhabit them – often for good, sometimes for ill. Universities especially, but all research institutions, face enormous economic, political, and sociological challenges in this decade. In striving to help their institutions meet these challenges, natural scientists, humanists, and social scientists all bear the responsibility to understand the ways in which their work impacts the lives of countless others, from students to colleagues to unknown millions who reap the consequences and moral dilemmas often born of academic research.

Chapter 7

Education and Schools

This chapter focuses on the impact of education on character formation, ethics, and the communication of values in late modern pluralistic societies. The placement of the education chapter in this volume – and, more important, the place of educational institutions in late modern pluralistic societies – requires some reflection. We have placed this discussion of education after the chapter on academic and scientific research, since today science and academic research in universities provide a significant framework for many educational processes today.

We could just as well have placed this chapter right after the opening chapter on the family, however. After all, historically and in many quarters still today the family remains the seedbed of personal education and the first school of character, values, and ethics. Indeed, in the introduction to this volume, we described a continuing process of differentiation of the so-called social systems or social spheres, starting with Martin Luther's doctrine of the three estates – the family, church, and state – and its antecedents. Aristotle and the Roman Stoics had already referred to the union of man and woman, the relationship of parents and children, and the institution of marriage and family as the basis of the polis. The Church Fathers and later the theologians of the Middle Ages, as well as legal scholars and philosophers in the following periods, saw the family as a religiously shaped community that also, in turn, shaped religion and was the seedbed of the institutions of public life, including schools. Luther had captured this idea in his famous three-estates doctrine.

However, we have chosen to arrange the chapters in this volume not in accordance with the three-estates doctrine with its impressive prehistory and development up to the present day. Rather, we charted our course by following the evolution of European universities, which began with three faculties of theology, law, and medicine, and later added the philosophical faculty as the fourth. Thus, our sequence of chapters has religion, law, medicine, and science come before the chapter of education. Moreover, with the exception of the family, we have concentrated throughout on large social organizations, such as the market, law, politics, media, science, religion, the military, and health care, which are indispensable for late modern pluralistic societies as a whole. To be sure, other associations and alliances of civil society, such as those involved in sports, arts, and aesthetics, are also extremely influential in shaping social terms and social norms, and they can have a great resonance and impact in many areas of social and ethical commitment. But we distinguish the ten enduring and indispensable social systems analyzed in this volume from the "plurality" of civil alliances and associations which tend to be more fluid, transient, and optional. In many parts of the world, as Australian bishop Stephen Pickard documents, formal systems of education and schooling are still optional civil associations, too.[171] But in late modern pluralistic societies in the West, education is an enduring and indispensable social system, and schools a critical buttress for individual flourishing, social cohesion, and the pursuit of truth, justice, peace, and order.

Our interdisciplinary research group that studied the moral impact of education includes scholars from four continents, representing a broad range of disciplines: theology and ethics, historical and pedagogical disciplines, psychology, political science, literary studies, anthropology, and law. They shed light on the religious, moral, and political influence on and of educational processes. And they illustrate the broad impact of education on children at different stages of their development, and the communication of values in different social contexts.

Religious and Psychological Resources for Education

Several members of our research team analyzed some of the religious and psychological sources and resources of the educational processes and their impact on character development and the transmission of values in contemporary societies. American theologian Anne Stewart poses the question, "What does Solomon have to do with Google?" Provocatively, she examines the potential of Old Testament wisdom literature to enhance the processes of truth-seeking in mod-

---

[171] See Stephen Pickard, introduction to Stephen Pickard, Michael Welker, and John Witte, Jr., eds. *The Impact of Education on Character Formation, Ethics, and the Communication of Values in Late Modern Pluralistic Societies* (Leipzig: Evangelische Verlangsanstalt, 2022) [hereafter *Education and Character*], 13–24. Pickard further makes the distinction between multisystemic, organized "pluralism", and a polyphonic "plurality" of individuals, groups, and social associations, which is also highly important for liberal societies.

ern pluralistic societies.[172] Focusing on the book of Proverbs, she shows how important it is to engage with different truth claims that compete or conflict with each other. In an environment of differing ideological perspectives and conflicting moral attitudes, it is also necessary to recognize and learn how to deal with socially influential "wishes and desires." The dangers of falsely controlling wishes and desires – for example, through monetization – the dangers of manipulating information, and the tendency to generate tensions and divisions in society out of external interests can be seen both in the life situations of Solomon's time and in our day. The book of Proverbs, Stewart shows, presents different voices of the "wise woman" or "woman of wisdom" and the "strange woman" and encourages the development of a wise character in different living conditions through ethical reflection on different life contexts. Striving for ethical orientation, knowledge of truth, and wisdom is not only a blessing for personal development but also a test of character development and ethos in a society.

American anthropologist Robert Hefner picks up on some of these same themes.[173] He asks what framework conditions must be in place in today's societies and political conditions for effective and conclusive character development. Which framework conditions promote, and which block, educational processes and influence the understanding of the public good? He sees obstacles to the formation of a sustainable social consensus in an ethical-religious diversity. In his opinion, new forms of social mobilization that create ethical and social differences out of commercial and political interests must be recognized and contained. With Charles Taylor and John Rawls, he is looking for an "overlapping consensus" that can support civic and civil society coexistence and interest in the common good.

Hefner concedes that some of the "central characteristics of Christianity", which he does not characterize in detail, have had significant negative social and ethical consequences for minorities, which he also does not characterize in detail. Nevertheless, he calls for recognizing the provision of "theological and ontological foundations for the Christian affirmation of human dignity." Hefner sees a danger in the form of "political entrepreneurs" in civil society who appeal to popular Christian identities through "political instrumentalization" in order to overshadow the messages of the Gospel that affirm universal human dignity. It is clear that he takes a rather negative view of the separation of powers in pluralistic societies, as this offers a gateway to exclusionary and

---

[172] Anne W. Stewart, "What Has Solomon to Do with Google? Old Testament Wisdom Literature and the Mediation of Truth in Modern Pluralistic Societies", in *Education and Character*, 25–35.

[173] Robert W. Hefner, "Character Socialization and Social Diversity in Modern Democracies Today", in *Education and Character*, 37–45.

noninclusive messages. However, he would like to see the inclusive messages guaranteed in a general and religious education.

German psychologist Joachim Funke presents several specialist studies on the interaction of psychology and education.[174] It is important to him to differentiate between different dynamics in people's life courses. In contrast to a long-practiced standard approach, which had generally considered the origins and developments of general moral values and their possible changes, he introduces two newer approaches: first, the view that character develops in connection with moral behavior over a lifetime, just as cognition, emotions, and language do, per Jean Piaget and Lawrence Kohlberg. On the other hand, Funke acknowledges a broader approach that links character development with personality development, taking into account both stable and variable phases in the course of life and its changing circumstances. Funke is skeptical of scholarship that seeks to measure concrete developmental processes in order to understand the complexity of character development. He sees the years-long search for values and meaning as an essential human activity whose goal should be to capture and appreciate the individual development of every person in society. The key questions are where and with whom and in which circles one should seek and find responsibility in order to develop and strengthen one's social skills and virtues.

American education specialist Charles Glenn takes up this question in his chapter on "civic and civil norms and distinctive beliefs."[175] Glenn examines the controversial significance of religious schools for general education. Do they pose a fundamental threat to social cohesion? Should they be excluded from general education processes? He warns against the "myth of a school for all" and quotes the skeptical voice of Michel Foucault that the modern state has taken over from the medieval church the role and techniques of "preserving souls for the maintenance of public peace and justice." Glenn describes the dangers of politicizing the education of children and young people. He asks how and by whom civil society and civic virtues could be developed and cultivated. He calls for examination and appreciation of the power of religious institutions (including schools) to form shared convictions and commitments, which are important resources for society as a whole.

---

[174] Joachim Funke, "Character Formation from a Psychological Perspective: The Search for Values, the Search for Meaning", in *Education and Character*, 47–58.

[175] Charles L. Glenn, "Civic Norms and Distinctive Convictions: Finding the Right Balance", in *Education and Character*, 59–85.

Education and Character Development in Comparative Perspective

Several other members of our research team examined educational processes and forms of character development in different national contexts: Germany, Australia, South Korea, and the United States.

German theologian Heike Springhart describes an incisive development in German postwar history.[176] Developed by numerous political, scientific, and church bodies in the United States, "reeducation programs" were carefully implemented for Germany and Japan after World War II. This meant reeducation and retraining as a pedagogical program, as a process of comprehensive democratization, and as the creation of spheres of individual and general education that were relatively unencumbered ideologically. The concept of "controlled institutional change", developed by Harvard sociologist Talcott Parsons, was influential. Democracy was seen as a way of life that should be made attractive and practiced through international cooperation and shared learning processes. Springhart focuses on the question of what roles religion and the church were able to play in this development. Protestant academies with their adult education programs in postwar Germany were of great importance, she shows, as were church-based diaconal institutions. Likewise, the increasingly important role of women in education and in the political realm of the newly forming society should not be underestimated.

Australian education professor Jo-Anne Reid examines the way school education in Australia has shaped character development and the nation.[177] She takes as her starting point persistent tensions between a systemic racism that had prevailed since Anglo-Saxon colonization of Australia in the late eighteenth century, but also countervailing developments that led to Australia becoming one of the most culturally and linguistically diverse societies. The development and maintenance of a value system for a pluralistic society was largely the responsibility of school education. With the help of a "decolonization curriculum" for each new generation of young Australians, the educational system opposed the emergence of numerous forms of discriminatory and undemocratic social conditions. Reid emphasizes the great importance of early childhood education, the indispensability of critically examining the various forms and costs of education, and, not least, persistent confrontation with a long history of ne-

---

[176] Heike Springhart, "Creating Continuity and Changing Spirituality: Germany's Democratization after 1945 as an Example of the Influence of Education on Character Development, the Transmission of Values, and the Collapse of Totalitarianism", in *Education and Character*, 107-22.

[177] Jo-Anne Reid, "School Education in Australia: Building Character and Reforming the Nation", in *Education and Character*, 123-46.

glect and oppression of indigenous peoples and the numerous difficulties wrought by political and educational countermeasures in this history of neglect.

The chapter by Korean scholar Chung-Hyun Baik offers an Asian perspective.[178] He describes, on one hand, the very high esteem in which school and university education is held in his country and, on the other hand, the strong emotional strain placed on students by the high expectations placed on them by their environments. He sees the roots of this tension in the country's long history of education. Despite various internal changes, the ironclad principle of meritocracy has been maintained. Not only academic, professional, and economic success in personal life, but also adherence to family values and obligations were closely linked to this performance mindset. Today's newer, more individualized perspectives on character development, ethical education, and contributions to the transmission of values in society are changing and weakening this orientation, which has long been focused on the family and traditional culture.

One of us (American jurist and legal historian John Witte) examines the "restoration" of the importance of religious values in American public education.[179] He observes an upheaval in many orientation processes following a new appreciation of the role of religion in the education system. The influence of the legal system and the various developments highlighted in the chapters herein on religion and law and the drastically changed relationship between these two social systems have contributed significantly to this upheaval. The view that religion is essentially a matter of private disposition and that it should be relegated to the fringes of public education has been fundamentally corrected. Recent political, religious, and legal developments in many countries have been observed and have led internationally to a flurry of research projects, publications, and new institutionalizations in the fields that can generally be summarized under the title "Law and Religion." These changes have contributed to the "restoration" of the importance of religious values in American public education.

American educator Ashley Berner turns to the latest developments in education in the United States.[180] Berner assumes that schools are meaning-identifying and meaning-articulating institutions and that a complex educational program is therefore necessary for students. In her opinion, even topics in school lessons that have negative connotations or are perceived as marginalized can

---

[178] Chung-Hyun Baik, "An Examination of the Influence of the Korean Education System on the Character, Ethics, and Values of Koreans and Its Impact on Late Modern Pluralistic Societies", in *Education and Character*, 147-53.

[179] John Witte, Jr., "Restoring the Value(s) of Religion in American Public Education", in *Education and Character*, 89-105.

[180] Ashley Berner, "Public Education and Moral Formation in the United States: A View from the Early Twenty-First Century", in *Education and Character*, 155-69.

have a formative effect. She opposes anxious attempts to make educational processes uniform under the pretext of "moral neutrality" or to launch uniform countermodels to existing constellations. She identifies several undesirable developments, including a problematic "moral therapeutic deism", on the one hand, and an "expressive individualism", on the other, as concentrating or dissociating attempts at uniformity in the models on offer. She makes an emphatic plea for pluralistic models of public education, as difficult and demanding as this task may be.

Old and New Challenges in Education

American religion professor David Cunningham calls for a better integration of education and vocation, in line with earlier Christian teachings on education.[181] Modern education should not be just about learning intellectual and technical skills, Cunningham argues. It should also be about cultivating and integrating the virtues and values needed for students to discover and develop their vocations in rich personal, civic, domestic, and political lives. By focusing on their distinct vocation, students are able to make choices and experience limits and finiteness in a world with an overwhelming abundance of life possibilities. But by enjoying a deep education, students are also able to appreciate different forms and methods of knowledge and a range of experiences in and from other national contexts. Cunningham calls for a kind of cosmopolitanism in modern education that produces students with historically and socially trained foresight to navigate the world and their place within it. With this approach, he aims to avoid unfruitful tensions between public secular universities – which want to stay away from religious or quasi-religious topics – and private, often religiously influenced educational institutions, and to build and maintain fruitful relationships between the two sides.

German literature professor Irene Pieper offers a contribution on the impact of literature on character development.[182] Concentrating on the formative powers of literature brings into view a broader emancipatory field with high relevance for personal and social life. She emphasizes the importance of literature as a critical catalyst in the processes of self-discovery for pupils and students, as well as in the search for their appropriate place and purpose in the world. Literature confronts and challenges political, moral, and aesthetic configurations, both in the societies in which we live and in societies and living conditions that

---

[181] David S. Cunningham, "Vocation Exploration as Character Formation: A New Direction in Higher Education", in *Education and Character*, 173–85.
[182] Irene Pieper, "Character Development and Literary Education: Goals and Potentials", in *Education and Character*, 187–200.

are distant in space and time. In this way, engaging with literature shapes and changes the way we live.

Literature makes people aware of neglected and suppressed possibilities for living and shaping life; it prevents an excessive fixation on local and current major problems and an absolutization of the respective *Zeitgeist*. However, Pieper also draws attention to the dangers of politically prescribed literature in general educational processes and the risks of precarious countermeasures. She finds it remarkable that the personal reading interests and reading habits of students and teaching staff are often very different when it comes to the texts required for school or university curricula. Finally, she addresses the power of surprise in the chosen literature and the role of enthusiasm on the part of the teaching staff. In all educational processes, it is crucial to awaken the joy of reading and discussion.

American psychologist Darcia Narvaez emphasizes the high responsibility of education in general and ethical education in particular in confronting the dramatic processes of global ecological endangerment and self-endangerment.[183] Narvaez calls for efforts to achieve a better understanding of global cultural development processes, the fostering of a nature-centered ethos, and an appreciation for the ways of life of indigenous peoples and populations. The question of an ecologically sustainable future must be placed at the center of education, Narvaez argues. Prevailing thought and established metaphors must be recognized and reviewed if moral, political, economic, and media routines are not to be continued. She warns against well-meaning but overly simplistic, dualistic critical approaches that seek to counteract a long-established ecological brutalism with moral recommendations. A thorough reorientation of education must begin with concern for early childhood health and emotional development.

Human development did not begin with civilization, as many Western thinkers like to claim, Narvaez concludes. She offers instead a romantic image of nature that, while compelling in the abstract, ignores the erratic and predatory aspects of nature. As a countermeasure against dominant driving forces in human history – she mentions "mercantilism, colonialism, and capitalism" – her objection is easy to understand. From the perspective of more differentiated perceptions of science, economics, law, and politics, however, her objection and the desire to return to pre-civilizational wisdom will make sense as an understandable defensive stance, (even a "prophetic" one, in Stephen Pickard's apt phrase[184]), but will also raise the question of whether it could serve as a comprehensive approach to solving the global ecological crisis.

---

[183] Darcia Narvaez, "Recasting the Starting Conditions for an Earth-Centered Ethical Education", in *Education and Character*, 201–13.

[184] Pickard, introduction to *Education and Character*, 22.

Chapter 8

The Market and Economics

Markets – like families, churches, and states – are ancient institutions in the Western tradition, and they are now at the heart of economies in late modern Western pluralistic societies, indeed, in most of the world. The word "economy" (*oikonomia*) originally denoted stewardship of the household and its members (the *oikos*), but it eventually covered the activities of planning, administration, and financial management in all institutions – from households and small shops to nations and empires. The word "market" (*mercātus*) originally meant the physical location for buying, selling, and trading goods, commodities, or services. Such physical markets still exist today, of course: think of weekend farmers' markets, summer fairs, or annual Christmas markets. So do visible locations of market activity: think of stores, malls, banks, or the trading floor of the New York Stock Exchange. But many markets today are virtual, invisible, even fictitious. They involve millions of often instant and invisible transactions, exchanges, and other economic activities among individuals and institutions at the local, regional, national, and global levels.[185]

Markets Are Essential Institutions

"Human lives everywhere" are suffused "with economic relationships", leading German economist Jürgen von Hagen writes. "Human beings live together, work

---

[185] Jürgen von Hagen, Michael Welker, John Witte, Jr., and Stephen Pickard, eds., *The Impact of the Market on Character Formation, Ethical Education, and the Communication of Values in Late Modern Pluralistic Societies* (Leipzig: Evangelische Verlagsanstalt, 2020) [hereafter *Market and Character*].

together, and share economic resources."[186] That makes markets a perennial and pervasive institution, deeply intertwined with individuals and groups. Indeed, all the other modern social institutions that we are analyzing in this volume – families, churches, states, schools, media, research, military, and healthcare institutions – depend on, participate in, and are affected by markets.

Both historically and today, markets have involved voluntary exchanges between buyers and sellers, each seeking to gain something from the transaction. While the dialectics of free markets versus regulated markets have long divided commentators and courts, markets have always needed at least a baseline of rules and regulations to function properly. As von Hagen notes, these rules ensure that "contracts and transactions are in the interest of society", that supply lines are filled, that prices and currencies remain relatively stable, that promises are kept, and that price-gouging, hoarding, collusion, fraud, and other market distortions are prohibited and punished.[187]

To be sure, feudal overlords, political tyrants, and economic tycoons over the centuries have sometimes captured, controlled, and corrupted some markets to their own great advantage and at great cost to the common good. But in late modern Western societies today, domestic and international legal authorities as well as sundry nonstate associations have created a complex network of market rules designed to ensure that markets make available at least the essential commodities and services that consumers need to survive, let alone flourish. And to be sure, markets offer all manner of excess goods, services, and activities that go far beyond what is necessary for survival – sometimes encouraging and facilitating pride, greed, wrath, envy, lust, gluttony, sloth, and many other sins. But modern pluralistic societies largely leave it to the consumer to choose among essential and nonessential offerings, even while state laws prohibit highly dangerous or offensive market behavior – say, selling babies or organs, peddling dangerous street drugs, or trafficking youngsters for sex. Outside of these contexts, "the proper functioning of markets depends on the character of those trading in them."[188]

Because of their perennial power and pervasiveness in human life and society, markets have attracted a long history of reflection in the Western tradition. Classical, biblical, Talmudic, and patristic teachings alike have set many of the basic premises for Western teachings on the morality of wealth, economic

---

[186] Jürgen von Hagen, "Old Testament Principles of Economic Ethics", in *Market and Character*, 133–46, at 133.
[187] Ibid., 133–35.
[188] Jurgen Von Hagen, "Markets and the Human Character", in *Market and Character*, 23–38, at 35.

justice, and household management.[189] Medieval and early modern jurists, ethicists, and canonists set many of the legal and moral rules governing trade, banking, wealth, and relief of the poor.[190] The rise of modern market economies has triggered a whole industry of deep scholarly engagement that figures prominently today in politics and economic policymaking, academic research and teaching, and business planning and market participation.[191]

Do Markets Encourage Moral Character Formation?

Many historical and modern figures have argued that markets encourage the cultivation of public and private morality and often positively impact human character and ethics. The rise of early modern market economies had helped to create increased prosperity, greater social mobility, and a wider optimism throughout much of Europe and its overseas colonies.[192] Many of the foundational texts of classical liberal economics, forged in this new optimistic era, argued that market societies promote more justice, fairer dealings, closer relations, and better social order than the earlier systems of feudalism or church-regulated markets. French philosopher Voltaire, for example, described the London Stock Exchange as a place "where the representatives of all nations meet for the benefit of mankind ... There the Presbyterian confides in the Anabaptist,

---

[189] See, for example, chapters by Michael J. Broyde, "Law, Economy, and Charity: Formations in Torah and Talmud", in *Market and Character*, 115–32; von Hagen, "Old Testament Principles of Economic Ethics"; Peter Lampe, "Christian-Apocalyptic Protest from the First-Century 90s as a Reaction to Economic Conditions", in *Market and Character*, 161–70; Kaja Wieczorek, "Economic Conditions Impacting Luke's Concept of Economic Solidarity", in *Market and Character*, 147–60; and Samuel Gregg, "Commerce, Finance, and Morality in the Thought of Early Modern Catholic Scholastics", in *Market and Character*, 171–87.

[190] See sources and discussion in Paul Oslington, ed., *The Oxford Handbook of Christianity and Economics* (Oxford: Oxford University Press, 2014) and numerous texts in the *Journal of Markets and Morality*.

[191] Piet Naudé, "A Conceptual Analysis of 'Value' in Select Business Literature and Its Implications for Ethical Educations", in *Market and Character*, 247–63, at 260. See further Piet Naudé, "'In God We Trust': Bringing Michael Welker into Conversation with *The Market as God* by Harvey Cox", in Heike Springhart and Günter Thomas, *Risko und Vertrauen / Risk and Trust: Festschrift für Michael Welker zum 70. Geburtstag* (Leipzig: Evangelische Verlangsanstalt, 2017), 223–40; and Jürgen von Hagen, "Economic Perspectives on Trust, Risk, and Uncertainty", in *Risk and Trust*, 207–22.

[192] Jürgen von Hagen, introduction to *Market and Character*, 15.

and the Churchman depends on the Quaker's word."[193] Scottish philosopher David Hume argued that the free exchange of goods, ideas, and technologies in an open market improved both the character and quality of life for most individuals and society.[194] French political philosopher Baron Montesquieu similarly argued:

> It is almost a general rule that commerce prevails where manners are gentle, and that manners are gentle where commerce prevails ... Commerce has a particular character which distinguishes it from the other professions in which men engage. It has such a singular influence on a man's feelings & inclinations, that from being haughty & proud, it suddenly makes him supple, binding & helpful. Through Commerce, man learns to think, to have probity & morals, to be cautious & reserved in his actions. Feeling the need to be wise & honest to succeed, he shuns vice, or at least if he has an exterior full of decency & gravity, so as not to make those who have an interest in knowing him judge badly of him; he would not dare to sit down for fear of damaging his credit; thus, Society does not suffer from a scandal which it might otherwise have to complain about.[195]

This conviction that markets encourage morality and positive moral character development has many modern champions. Dutch-born sociologist Frank J. Lechner, for example, has defended "the market's moral merits", arguing that capitalist commercial activity cultivates the classical and Christian virtues of courage, temperance, justice, prudence, faith, hope, and love. Pursuing self-interest in such an economy is inherently virtuous, Lechner argues in line with classical economic teachings, because it demands prudence and attention to what the other wants and needs – a kind of economic "golden rule" of doing unto others as they would do for themselves. Likewise, entrepreneurship can be said to embody hope and courage, while loyal work reflects temperance and faith. "[T]he modern moral order revolves around individuals freely exchanging for mutual benefit, and that *leitmotif* naturally favored the economy as the sphere in which to realize that benefit."[196]

Reacting to the common charge that markets foster selfishness, greed, and materialism, American economist Jason Brennan has argued that selfishness is

---

[193] Voltaire, "Letter VI: On the Presbyterians", in *Letters Concerning the English Nation*, trans. John Lockman (London: Peter Davis, 1926 [1733]), 34.

[194] David Hume, "Of Commerce" (1752) in id., *Essays: Moral, Political, and Literary* (New York: Cosimo, 2007 [1903-04]), 259-75.

[195] Baron de Montesquieu, *The Spirit of Laws* (1748), trans. Thomas Nugent (New York: Colonial Press, 1899), bk. 20, chaps. 1-2.

[196] Frank J. Lechner, "Commercial Society and Its Values: The Merit of the Market in Social Theory", in *Market and Character*, 39-50, at 44.

more common in nonmarket societies than in market societies. "In general, people from market-based economies seem to have adopted a tendency to empathize with strangers and exhibit a stronger sense of fairness than people from nonmarket societies."[197] Economists Ginny Seung Choi and Virgil Henry Storr have pressed this case empirically. They compared extensive data drawn from international studies that measured tendencies toward selfishness versus selflessness, honesty versus dishonesty, and loyalty versus disloyalty in economic actors. Their data indicate that market economies generally fared better in nurturing positive, other-regarding traits compared to nonmarket economies.

Brennan, Choi, and Storr all concede that market economies do attract their share of morally questionable individuals, fraudulent cads, and occasional massively corrupt entrepreneurs – think of Bernie Madoff and his multibillion-dollar Ponzi scheme. But their data suggest that market economies, at the very least, do not encourage morally inferior social behavior. Moreover, the public and private regulations of these markets – together with the glaring democratic spotlight that social media now can shine on bad actors to their great economic and social loss – do deter and punish bad market behavior.[198] "[I]f markets truly systematically favored and rewarded the wealthy, the greedy, the frauds, and the heartless, there would be genuine concerns about the free reign of markets in our society and genuine reasons to restrict the free operation of markets. Fortunately, this concern seems to be moot. At worst, it appears that markets do not promote misbehavior any more than alternative economic systems do."[199]

Are Markets Amoral?

For the past century, most academic economists have ignored the impact of markets on moral character formation. Economists are focused on the market alone, while "the influence of this coordination system on values and norms [are] considered outside the scope of economic science."[200] "All that an economist can claim about a market ... is that it yields an efficient allocation of resour-

---

[197] Jason Brennan, "How Market Society Affects Character", in *Market and Character*, 73–92, at 79–80.

[198] Ginny Seung Choi and Virgil Henry Storr, "Growing Up in the Market: The Character Traits that Markets Reward and Punish", in *Market and Character*, 51–72, at 55.

[199] Ibid., 71.

[200] Annemiek Schilpzand and Eelke de Jong, "Do Market Societies Undermine Civic Morality? An Empirical Investigation into Market Societies and Civic Morality Across the Globe", *Journal of Economic Behavior & Organization* 208 (Apr. 2023): 39–60.

ces in a precise way."[201] This is standard economic lore from most academic economists. To be sure, in recent years, some behavioral economists have studied how nature and nurture, biology and society influence a person's rational choices.[202] Other economists have studied the effects of market forces on moral attitudes and behaviors through the evaluation of tools like the Economic Freedom Index.[203] But these new scholarly accents among some recent economists have not changed the dominant economic narrative that markets are amoral, and that economics must focus on profit, efficiency, cost-benefit analysis, rational choice, and individual freedom.

American Nobel economist Milton Friedman long championed this argument that free markets are amoral. "Only people can have responsibilities", he wrote, while "'business' as a whole cannot be said to have responsibilities." A free market "gives people what they want instead of what a particular group thinks they ought to want. Underlying most arguments against the free market is a lack of belief in freedom itself" and with it the critical proposition that moral choices should be left with the individual. Friedman dismissed most moral arguments surrounding economic behavior and market policy as little more than statements of preference akin to choosing among flavors of ice cream. "In a free society, it is hard for ›good‹ people to do ›good‹, but that is a small price to pay for making it hard for 'evil' people to do 'evil', especially since one man's good is another's evil."[204] While he acknowledged the need for market laws against force and fraud, he insisted that questions of morality and character in the market and other economic spheres should be left to the individual participants and whatever other associations of which they are part.

---

[201] Dani Rodrik, *Economics Rules: The Rights and Wrongs of the Dismal Science* (New York: W. W. Norton, 2014), 105.

[202] See Klaus Mathis and Ariel David Steffen, "From Rational Choice to Behavioral Economics: Theoretical Foundations, Empirical Findings and Legal Implications", in *European Perspectives on Behavioural Law and Economics,* ed. Klaus Mathis (Heidelberg: Springer International, 2015), 31–48.

[203] See discussion in Brennan, "How Market Society Affects Character." See also Niclas Berggren, "The Benefits of Economic Freedom: A Survey", *The Independent Review* 8 (Fall, 2003), 193–211; and Jeremy Jackson and Scott Beaulier, "Economic Freedom and Philanthropy", *Journal of Economic Behavior & Organization* 214 (Oct. 2023): 148–83.

[204] Milton Friedman, "A Friedman Doctrine: The Social Responsibility of Business Is to Increase Its Profits", *New York Times* (Sep. 13, 1970), Section SM, p. 17; Milton Friedman, *Capitalism and Freedom* [1962], 40th Anniversary Edition (Chicago: University of Chicago Press, 2002), 15.

German philosopher Rüdiger Bittner likewise rejects the idea that market economies and liberal capitalism more generally are moral or immoral or have a bearing on moral formation or ethical education. Bittner writes:

> It is not through our [market or] political economy that characters are formed and values transmitted. Liberal capitalism is morally neutral, for as long as it is liberal it presents to people a whole range of courses to take. What makes them think of good and bad the way they do is not liberal capitalism, but the particular experience they go through within liberal capitalism. In response to the human beings they meet and the events through which they live, they come to see things this way or that way and direct their steps in the future. So if we want to improve character formation and value transmission, we should not worry about liberal capitalism. We should see to it that within liberal capitalism people find sufficient space to appreciate or to reject, as they think fit, the human paths that our culture offers.[205]

Do Markets Harm Moral Character Formation?

While many scholars and policy makers consider markets to be morally neutral, if not morally positive, some modern critics argue that modern economic markets trade in false methodologies and assumptions that ultimately encourage immoral behavior and distort ethics and character formation. Australian Anglican Bishop Stephen Pickard, for example, has sharply criticized the false anthropology of market economics. He takes aim at the reductive image of the "economic man" (*homo economicus*) constantly bent on maximizing benefits and minimizing costs and making rational choices accordingly. This view of human nature certainly explains and predicts some aspects of our commercial and economic behavior, Pickard allows. After all, most of us shop for bargains, buy things on sale, and invest our hard-earned income in retirement funds that balance decent returns and tolerable risks. But cost-benefit analysis does not and should not describe and dominate many other aspects of our lives, Pickard continues – particularly our family lives, community service, charitable giving, artistic motivations, aesthetic decisions, religious commitments, and so much more. Privileging rational and utilitarian choices for enduring human interactions and conscientious living deprecates the richness and complexity of motivations and inspirations beyond mere self-interest – not least those of faith, hope, and love. And the idea of *homo economicus* offers only a bleak and "trun-

---

[205] Rüdiger Bittner, "Our Political Economy's Moral Teaching", in Piet Naudé, Michael Welker, and John Witte, Jr. eds., *The Impact of Political Economy on Character Formation, Ethical Education, and the Communication of Values in Late Modern Pluralistic Societies* (Leipzig: Evangelische Verlagsanstalt, 2023) [hereafter *Political Economy and Character*], 137–49, at 149.

cated version of the virtuous human agent operating within a complex life world [that] is insufficient to generate the optimal conditions for the nurture of virtue and the formation of character that might contribute to the well-being and good of society and the planet." Pickard calls for "a more realistic anthropology" that predicates all human relationships, even economic interactions, on the fundamental virtues of trust, cooperation, and the common good.[206]

Similarly, Australian Christian economist Paul Oslington has warned against the spillover effort of modern economic thought that is so narrowly centered on rational choice and utility-maximizing behavior. This caricature of human activity threatens other traditional notions of virtue and the pursuit of intrinsic goods, which for millennia had been taken as invaluable – even if these pursuits could not be regarded efficient, rational, or wealth-maximizing. "Most economists see rationality only as a tool for explaining and predicting" human behavior, Oslington argues. They pretend that they do not make "any normative claims" or value judgments but are merely providing "a neutral set of tools." The problem is that economists have applied their "economic teaching on behavior" well beyond the commercial, business, and labor sphere, often eclipsing other "virtues and values that are so essential to moral character and ethical deliberation."[207]

Oslington's worries are well taken. Everything from picking your spouse to choosing your vocation to selecting your faith are all now subjects of whole libraries of economic guides to the most effective and efficient ends. Several studies, for example, now compare the relative costs and benefits of pursuing Jewish, Islamic, Catholic, and Protestant pathways to salvation – with "justification by faith alone" easily the most efficient. Some rational-choice theorists have also taken their calculus into the intimate sphere of sex, marriage, and family life and argued for the freedom to choose prostitution, polygamy, incest, open marriage, à la carte family forms, "take-out" sperm banks, free-market artificial reproductive technology, surrogacy, adoption, baby selling, and more. American political philosopher Michael J. Sandel laments this economic reductionism in his book, *What Money Can't Buy:*

---

[206] Stephen Pickard, "Rational Choice Theory and Virtuous Economics", in *Market and Character*, 233–46, esp. 240–42. See further Sergio Belardinelli, "Social Systems, Moral Individualism, and Education", in *Political Economy and Character*, 101–14.

[207] Paul Oslington, "Understanding the Economic Impacts of Virtue and the Pursuit of Good", in *Market and Character*, 93–114, at 96–97. See further Paul Oslington, "Why Is the Conversation Between Theologians and Economists So Difficult?" in *Political Economy and Character*, 115–36.

> In its own way, market reasoning ... empties public life of moral argument. Part of the appeal of markets is that they don't pass judgment on the preferences they satisfy. They don't ask whether some ways of valuing goods are higher, or worthier, than others. If someone is willing to pay for sex or a kidney, and a consenting adult is willing to sell, the only question the economist asks is, "How much?" Markets don't wag fingers. They don't discriminate between admirable preferences and base ones. Each party to a deal decides for himself or herself what value to place on the things being exchanged. This nonjudgmental stance toward values lies at the heart of market reasoning and explains much of its appeal.[208]

South African business school dean Piet Naudé has argued that the uncritical adoption of neoclassical economic thinking in business education has led too many graduates to think that business and market activities are objective and inherently amoral. Several cross-cultural empirical studies, Naude writes, have shown how the repeated and uncritical use of the *homo economicus* ideal, together with the strong competitiveness of business school education altogether, has inclined students and graduates toward a reductive ethic of self-interest. This has contributed significantly to a narrowing of moral character formation and the communication of values in the business world, with detrimental consequences for financial markets, international cooperation, and the natural environment.

Business education has never been value-neutral, Naudé argues, and attempting to separate it from underlying implicit values of neoliberalism is philosophically unsound. Prioritizing economic value and privileging profit-making for businesses reflects specific views about human nature and motivations, which "are in themselves significant moral choices already."[209] Naudé and other scholars like Australian jurist Nicholas Aroney thus call for a reconceptualization of business education as well as legal education that aims to embed a range of values in the curriculum and provide a normative framework for the entire education process of budding professionals.[210]

---

[208] Michael J. Sandel, *What Money Can't Buy: The Moral Limits of Markets* (New York: Farrar, Straus, and Giroux, 2012), 11.

[209] Piet Naudé, "A Conceptual Analysis of 'Value' in Select Business Literature and Its Implications for Ethical Educations", in *Market and Character*, 247–62.

[210] Ibid.; and Nicholas Aroney, "Economics, Law, Education, and Religion – Contributions to the Composition of the Good Society", in *Political Economy and Character*, 81–100.

Concluding Reflections

Markets are perennial institutions in human society, providing essential (and sometimes excess) goods, services, and opportunities. Without markets, human living would be reduced to an endless daily and dangerous pursuit of hunting and gathering of the minima needed to survive. This is lamentably the condition still suffered by some chronically poor and needy members of affluent societies, let along the many millions today devastated by war, famine, and other natural or human tragedies or living in refugee camps or in corrupt or broken nations around the world. But in late modern pluralistic liberal societies, stable markets are designed to ensure that most people get at least their "daily bread" – with private charity, diaconal support, and state welfare systems supporting those with too little.

Churches in the past, and states and industry regulators today, set basic guidelines to ensure that markets function efficiently and that market participants honor their promises and desist from patently immoral behavior and trade. In that sense, markets do set a baseline of minimal economic morality and a platform for exposing fraudsters, cheats, and criminals. Moreover, when they are open and fair, markets provide endless opportunities for individuals to share the fruits of their honest labor and vocations, and to acquire and distribute the goods and services needed to support loved ones and dependents. Markets are not monitors and makers of morality; that is left to market participants themselves and the other social institutions (including families and churches) of which they are a part.[211] But markets do provide individuals and institutions with the freedom and opportunity to express their moral choices and ethical preferences through buying and selling, advertising and advocating, donating and distributing goods, services, ideas, and information.

Many academic economists today consider markets themselves to be amoral. But many of these same economists also champion a distinct moral view of the rational *homo economicus* bent on making the most efficient and effective choices to maximize profits. That anthropology, which is relentlessly drilled into students of business, has spilled over into many areas of life beyond market activity, including decisions about our faith, family, health care, education, academic research, media, military choices, and much more. Critics from various fields, including notably theology, ethics, sociology, and public policy, have pushed back on this bleak *homo economicus* caricature of human nature. They have called for a robust return to norms of moral formation and forms of ethical calculus that take much more seriously the virtues and values of faith, hope,

---

[211] Andreas Glaeser, "Ethics' Political Imperative: Moving toward Better Institutions", in *Political Economy and Character*, 45–66.

and love, and of justice, mercy, and peace. It is those virtues and values that ultimately make our human lives worth living, including our economic lives.

Chapter 9

Media and Communication

While forms and norms of communication have marked human societies from the very beginning, our project has focused on the moral and ethical impact of mass media, the print press, radio and television, the film industry, and the internet and social platforms that have come into existence more recently.[212] The authors of the interdisciplinary volume to emerge from this study show how strongly these media set in motion the communication of values through selective processes; how a limited selection of values is privileged; and how ethical prejudices and biases are generated. All of these processes in turn have had an enormous impact on moral character development and ethical education in large sections of the population in late modern pluralistic societies – and well beyond as well.

The four parts of the volume begin with the first section asking the question: In what ways are the mass media of particular importance for the communication of values in modern pluralistic societies? The second part delves into media economics and the ethical implications of the strong interdependencies between media and economic processes. The third part examines the influence of the media on the development and change of ethical values in late modern societies. The fourth part is dedicated to specific ethical problems in mass media communication.

---

[212] Michael Welker, Jürgen von Hagen et al., eds., *The Impact of the Media on Character Formation, Ethical Education, and the Communication of Values in Late Modern Pluralistic Societies* (Leipzig: Evangelische Verglagsanstalt; Eugene, OR: Wipf & Stock, 2022) [hereafter *Media and Character*].

In the first part of the book, "Media and Values", German theologian and sociologist Günter Thomas offers a fundamental contribution on the topic.[213] He argues that the term "media society" best describes the prevailing modes of action and working methods of contemporary societies in the West. Media communication processes not only permeate the organization of other social systems or social spheres in late modern societies, they also exert enormous influence on everyday life and private spheres. The associated complexity and confusion pose a major challenge for individual orientation and social control processes.[214]

In his reflections, Günter Thomas is guided by the sociological, system-theoretical, and social-theoretical work of the brilliant thinker Niklas Luhmann (1927–1998). Luhmann distinguishes between four types of media: communication media, which are the basis of all social life; media of technological dissemination of communication, which are detached from direct personal communication and thus enable communication across large ranges in space and time; specific "symbolically generalized" media, which are linked to so-called social subsystems, such as those presented in this volume and series – economy, politics, law, religion, science, education, family, health care, and others; and, finally, the generalized media system, which spread in the twentieth century as a force and variable independent of the subsystems.

Thomas describes ten fields of media ethics that deal with these four types. He warns against the impression that people today are merely helpless observers of this complex media power. He encourages a double hermeneutic process in which people see themselves as responsible controllers and ask critically and self-critically about their own value preferences: What ideas of a good, just, and fruitful life determine our thoughts and actions? And further, what ideas of a good, just, and fruitful life are the most effective development trends in media practices? We should critically and self-critically examine the extent to which these value processes can mutually strengthen or weaken and block each other.

In this (and a second) chapter, Thomas discusses the struggles to gain and maintain attention in media societies. Organized sport, politics, religion, civil society, business, science, and education and many other areas compete for personal and public attention. Many dreams of achieving social harmony and understanding are linked to the fixation on attention. Unfortunately, however, gen-

---

[213] Günter Thomas, "The Texture of Values in the Media of Media Society: Preliminary Observations", in *Media and* Character, 23–46. See also Günter Thomas, *Medien. Ritual. Religion. Zur religiösen Funktion des Fernsehens* (Frankfurt am Main: Suhrkamp, 1998).

[214] Niklas Luhmann, *The Reality of the Mass Media* [1995], 5th ed. (Wiesbaden: Springer, 2017); and id., *Soziale Systeme. Grundriss einer allgemeinen Theorie* [1987], 18th ed. (Frankfurt: Suhrkamp, 2021).

erating media attention can also deepen conflicts, provoke hatred, consolidate self-isolation in communication bubbles, and serve to spread fake news. The possibilities of controlling and manipulating human thought, feeling, and behavior are frightening. All attempts to counteract these possibilities through intensive moral communication alone remain inadequate.

The second part of the book, "Media, Economics, and Ethics", delves more deeply into the observation of the problems of media power in the media society, and into the observation of the problems that media power creates in the media society. Taking on these problems, German economic experts Jürgen von Hagen and Matthias Vollbracht portray media markets as two-sided markets.[215] Media companies sell content to consumers. But media companies also offer providers access to potential buyers of their products. As the latter commerce is economically more successful, media companies concentrate more on increasing the number of their consumers than on maintaining the quality of their content. They focus on content and topics that the largest possible number of people find interesting and attention-grabbing. This focus limits the range of topics, values, and ethical communications that can be conveyed in a resonance-oriented manner.

Around 2010, the media markets were reconfigured by the intensification of internet use and social networks such as Facebook and Twitter. The production of media content of good technical quality is now possible for many people at low cost. Consequently, the volume and breadth of content is increasing dramatically. At the same time, the use of cookies and algorithms gives media companies the opportunity to collect vast amounts of information about the preferences and habits of individual consumers. This in turn offers great economic value, as it provides businesses with opportunities to successfully advertise and sell their products to specific consumers. The floods of information and consumer incentives released by the media mean that consumer attention is becoming a scarce and contested commodity.

The second article by Günter Thomas is dedicated to this topic.[216] He not only describes the disputes over contested cultural possessions and resources. He also notes that Christian communities and churches in particular should see themselves as places where important cultural resources of attention are renewed, refocused, cultivated, and invested outside of contemporary economic interests. Not only natural but also cultural resources require constant attention and care.

---

[215] Jürgen von Hagen and Matthias Vollbracht, "Media Economics: Overview and Recent Developments", in *Media and Character*, 49–75.

[216] Günter Thomas, "Clicks, Likes and Cookies: The Trade in Active and Potential Attention in Media-Saturated Societies", in *Media and Character*, 77–103.

Following various scientific attempts to deal constructively with the great expansion of the media in late modern pluralistic societies, Thomas recommends distinguishing attention from mere perception, setting out a typology of what he calls "reflexive attention", "empathetic and perceptive attention", "communicative attention", and "accumulated attention." He then describes the role of attention as a resource in communication theories and various strategies for attracting and manipulating attention. He reflects on strategies of constructing scarcity, new strategies of capturing attention beyond the strategies of conventional communication processes, the replacement of the use of money by market-relevant attention, and the organization of social forgetting. The chapter ends with reflections on the possible role of religion in these processes and on the tasks of the churches in an ecology of attention. An appreciation of the real polyphony of life and the question of human responsibility for the consumption of one's own media experiences should be taken seriously through the "extravagances" of the practices of faith, hope, and love. In these practices, prevailing economies of restless media attention can be scrutinized and changed.

The enormous market power that social networks have gained in the new media world has led many to ask how this market power can be regulated. French media and business expert Katrin Gülden Le Maire poses this question in her chapter.[217] She begins with an overview of the development of audiovisual media in modern democracies and their rise to a "fourth power or fourth estate" alongside the executive (administration), the legislature (parliament), and the judiciary (judiciary). She focuses particularly on the interdependencies of media power and political power and on the demanding ethos that politically independent journalists must develop. Without this ethos of media professionals, social networks operate by giving individuals and organizations opportunities to distribute and exchange information. They weaken the fourth estate of traditional media by redirecting the economic forces of business. Law, politics, and public opinion in civil society must focus on this market power of an essential infrastructure of society. How can this power be regulated legally, politically, and ethically and protected from abuse and uncontrolled growth?

The third part, "Media, Values, and Crises", focuses on the influence of the media on the development of ethical values. Nick Couldry, professor of media and communications at the London School of Economics, raises an alarm in his chapter.[218] He uses the term "datafied media" to warn that most human activities on the Internet are only permitted – with or without the knowledge and consent of the actors (!) – because they can be registered and traced. They are

---

[217] Katrin Gülden Le Maire, "Are Social Networks Media? The Problematic Financial Classification as 'Media Service Companies'" in *Media and* Character, 105–18.

[218] Nick Couldry, "Datafied Media and the Silent Derangement of Ethics", in *Media and Character*, 121–35.

registered as data that has potential economic value for the entities interested in them. Based on this observation, Couldry asks how datafied media affect character development and ethical education in contemporary societies. In doing so, he uses a broad concept of education.

Based on Aristotle and neo-Aristotelianism, he understands education as a process in which people enter into traditional historical processes of rational and ethical reflection on the world, and follow tested and proven traditions while exercising creative intellectual skills. He emphasizes the high relevance of the development of personal profiles in the living interaction between human individuals. And he asks what happens when very rapid developments in artificial intelligence and machine learning, driven by economic imperatives and fed by a data industry, displace this vibrant diversity of concrete human interactions. Couldry is very concerned about the loss of high qualities of humanity and ethos, a loss that he associates with a disruption of "communicative symmetry." Communicative symmetry is essentially guaranteed in person-to-person communication. If it is missing, connections to the good driving forces of history and tradition are jeopardized, and an immense loss of human control of individual and communal developments becomes imminent. Although he warns against hasty negative reactions to this development, he sees an urgent need to develop a media-critical ethic that addresses these cultural challenges.

New York-based sociologists Julia Sonnevend and Olivia Steiert offer an ambivalent picture of recent media developments.[219] They argue that this crisis in particular brings into focus the power of the media in contemporary social life, but also the limits of this power. They begin with reflections on the question of what it means to identify or construct an "event", and they shed light on the complex roles that journalists play in this process. Journalists not only inform, investigate, and analyze facts and events, Sonnevend and Steiert show; they also mobilize people, support the rights of minorities, amplify important voices and controversial topics, awaken and intensify solidarity, and support a variety of viewpoints and perspectives. With these diverse activities, journalists at their best can provide models for democratically relevant communication and life processes. In this way, they shape complex world views and launch real or ideal role models.

However, some journalists not only open up central and broad perspectives on reality, but can also restrict or even block such perspectives, and not only through intentional or unintentional misinformation. What are reliable facts and what is fake news? When can visual presentations trigger constructive feelings, and when do they arouse false feelings, uncertainty, a sense of catastro-

---

[219] Julia Sonnevend and Olivia Steiert, "Observing a Crisis through the Media: Reporting on the Coronavirus Pandemic in the Early Twenty-First Century", in *Media and Character*, 137–49.

phe, joy or fear? The authors speak of a "drama of misinformation" and "alternative facts", emphasize the great importance of reliable truth claims, and the equally great importance of constantly checking them. These aspirations have become even more pressing in our day of instant communication through the internet and other social media, and with the growing use of artificial intelligence, cybercrime, and data manipulation for sinister political and ideological ends.

South African-based philosopher Bert Olivier, like Nick Couldry, laments the growing loss of intensive person-to-person communication in late modern media societies.[220] This loss is accompanied by growing objectification of persons and things, and inadequate differentiation of orientations and decisions respecting them. This loss of differentiation often goes hand-in-hand with weakened emotional engagement and emotional involvement between persons. With these detachments, many people in late modern media societies have become obsessively fixated on large and small screens and consumed with a restless desire for "hyperconnectivity." For many today, particularly younger adults, the number of "followers", "fans", and "likes" on various social media now are taken as important measures of a person's self-worth, social influence, and cultural importance, even if none of these are based on any interpersonal contact or relationships. Like many other authors in this series on character formation, Olivier asks for sustainable concepts of education to strengthen the performance of schools and universities and to offer new forms of community and interpersonal communication. He sees robust "in-person" education as a counterforce in this gloomy depiction of contemporary cultures to awaken aesthetic joy and enthusiasm and to strengthen individual and shared longing. He draws on great theological classics such as Augustine, philosophers such as Martin Heidegger and Jean-Luc Nancy, as well as psychoanalysts such as Jacques Lacan.

Part four is entitled "Ethical Potentials and Problems in Media Communication." It examines specific potentials in media and political communication – for example, in connection with moral communication and successful mass media film offerings. Australian television expert James Mairata shows, in his chapter, that from early on, films were seen as important channels for conveying ethical norms, and that standardized forms were developed for this purpose.[221] It was important, for example, that good had to fight against evil. The historical examples of this trope go back to the oldest surviving murals in the world, the cave paintings of Lascaux in France, which date back between seventeen thousand

---

[220] Bert Olivier, "Contemporary Media and the Crisis of Values", in *Media and* Character, 152–66.

[221] James Mairata, "Why Moral Agency Is Crucial to Mainstream Cinema", in *Media and Character*, 170–78.

and thirty-eight thousand years. The moral impulses in modern films move between those for emotionality recommended by Hume and other authors and the appeals to rationality in the wake of philosophies such as Kant's. These and other interplays are intended to arouse and maintain the audience's engagement and attention. The audience should develop their own moral judgments about what they see, but also correct and change them. Moral learning processes are thus stimulated and communicated through film.

The South African contribution by Lizette Rabe offers a morally negative example with regard to women working in South African media.[222] She reports on how women are systematically discriminated against in South African society. The factual experiences conflict with the officially recognized values of fairness and gender equality. Two theoretical approaches – feminism and the theory of media hegemony – serve Rabe as a point of reference. She reports that female journalists are affected much more than their male colleagues by sexual harassment, physical threats, and attacks online. South African institutions, which have the task of protecting women against such pressures, often fail to do so. Despite official statements to the contrary, women in South Africa and the global South in general are often disadvantaged and threatened by violence and unfair treatment. Rabe therefore calls for a new reflection on the roles and rights of women and their positions – not only in the media – in late modern pluralistic societies.

German journalist Bodo Hombach concludes this study of the role of media and communication in moral formation and ethical education.[223] He appeals to television journalists and emphasizes the need to maintain high ethical standards. To ensure this, journalists must constantly scrutinize their own arguments and hypotheses and expect that their hypotheses will not hold up and will have to be changed in light of new facts. Good journalists must also keep their distance from the issues they report on and not be directly involved in practical ethical commitments. It is their duty to become sensitive to all possible forms of manipulation and to resist them. He sees a real danger in the fact that journalism increasingly aims to motivate emotionally rather than inform as objectively as possible. Journalists must not abandon their efforts to be objective, to deal with facts correctly, to be neutral, and to search for the truth if they want to carry out their task seriously in democratic and pluralistic societies.

---

[222] Lizette Rabe, "Trolls and Bullies: A South African Case Study of Cyber-Misogyny and the Media", in *Media and Character*, 179–203.

[223] Bodo Hombach, "'Attitude' Can Damage Attitude When Journalists Abuse Their Power", in *Media and Character*, 207–12.

Chapter 10

The Military and Character Formation[224]

Military land and naval forces have been a staple of organized societies from the beginning, joined in the last century by airpower. Historically, the military's primary function was to safeguard the territory and people within a state's jurisdiction and to defend against and respond to external threats.[225] More recently, three main factors have caused a significant shift in military action: (1) the transformation of political structures, (2) the limitations imposed by civil society, and (3) the development of autonomous weapons systems. Militaries are now responsible for a wider range of assignments beyond traditional combat, reflecting the complex relationship between military operations and modern societal values.

The introduction of advanced technologies has further ushered in a new era of military strategy shadowed by ethical complexities. These innovations offer strategic advantages in intelligence, surveillance, and risk mitigation, but they simultaneously challenge conventional notions of accountability and the moral underpinnings of warfare. Cyber operations, for example, blur the lines of state sovereignty and jurisdiction and require a reassessment of the nature, purpose, and limits of digital and virtual conflict. Similarly, the deployment of drones raises pivotal questions about actions taken in remote combat scenarios. It is essential to examine the implications of these technologies and to tailor

---

[224] We gratefully acknowledge the excellent work on this chapter by Madeline Muhlherr, JD Candidate and Woodruff Scholar in Law at Emory University.

[225] See Michael J. Walzer, *Just and Unjust Wars: A Moral Argument with Historical Illustrations,* 5th ed. (New York: Basic Books, 2015), 41. See also Torsten Meireis, "After Chivalry", in Stephen Pickard, Michael Welker, and John Witte, Jr., eds., *The Impact of the Military on Character Formation, Ethical Education, and the Communication of Values in Late Modern Pluralistic Societies* (Leipzig: Evangelische Verlagsanstalt, 2022), 123–40 (hereafter *Military and Character*).

military ethics to meet contemporary challenges. As German bishop and professor Jochen Cornelius-Bundschuh writes:

> The technological development of weapons has repeatedly called into question the ethical justification of military action. This is still true today with regard to nuclear, biological, and chemical weapons; it is particularly true at present with regard to the question of the use of so-called lethal autonomous weapon systems. In these systems, it is no longer one or more humans who decide on the selection of targets and the use of weapons, but an algorithm.[226]

The globalization of military engagement has also expanded the military's remit and required new introspective approaches to operations. Soldiers now regularly find themselves in missions that appear to blend combat and civilian aid. They must act not only as warriors but also as diplomats, nation builders, and agents of humanitarian relief, all of which requires a more nuanced understanding of their varied duties. As a result, modern soldiers must be more than honorable and brave; they must exhibit moral courage, astute judgment, and a heightened sense of responsibility.[227]

Ethical decision-making in the military transcends legality and obedience, demanding an appreciation of each military mission's moral landscape. Recognizing that legal compliance does not inherently guarantee ethical action is crucial to balancing tactical objectives with humanitarian concerns. As militaries navigate these obstacles, ethical conduct – rooted in an understanding of both historical precedents and the moral challenges of the present – remains vital. This conduct is foundational to maintaining the trust and legitimacy afforded to the military by society.[228]

Thus, warfare in the current era reveals not just technological and strategic shifts but also moral predicaments that must be addressed with thoughtfulness and responsibility. The military, as a critical global institution, is tasked with managing these issues with discernment and integrity. By fostering a culture of ethical reflection and addressing the present-day realities of conflict, the military reaffirms its dedication to the highest standards of conduct. Upholding core values – such as the importance of family, faith, and freedom – highlights its role in defending the nation's physical security and ethical integrity. The devel-

---

[226] Jochen Cornelius-Bundschuh, "The Military Defense System and the Public Soul in Germany", in *Military and Character*, 27–38, at 36.

[227] Marco Hofheinz, "The Indispensability of Virtues in the Military: Virtue Ethical Considerations Following the Guiding Concept of the *Miles Protector*", in *Military and Character*, 79–92.

[228] Hartwig von Schubert, "Which Morals Society Should Learn from the Military, and Which Decidedly Not", in *Military and Character*, 61–78.

opment of character and soldierly virtues affirms adherence to the principles of justice and peace and secures the military's moral authority and legitimacy on the international stage.

Character Formation and Soldierly Virtues

Today's soldiers are expected to possess the physical and strategic skills necessary to carry out their duties, as well as the ability to exercise discretion and make ethical judgments in difficult situations. As a result, the "professional and technical training of soldiers must be complemented by ethical training."[229] This level of preparedness ensures that the individual actions of military personnel reflect the core values of civil society. German systematic theologian Marco Hofheinz puts it pithily:

> Virtues cannot be commanded. Virtues must be learned. This requires a learning community, which in turn establishes a formative context of practice. For this reason, training, education, and living together in the armed forces must be designed in such a way that they serve to acquire and deepen virtues.[230]

Military training is known for its rigorous discipline and structured hierarchies. Within this controlled environment, servicemen and women are instilled with a core set of values such as courage, loyalty, integrity, and an unwavering sense of duty. These values are essential for navigating the complexities of warfare and peacekeeping efforts that military personnel face in action. Therefore, military preparedness focuses on acquiring moral character and personal responsibility as well as physical strength and tactical skills.

The *Miles Protector*

The concept of the *miles protector* (the soldier protector) captures the evolution of the soldier's role from a pure combatant to a guardian of peace and stability as well. The modern soldier must be able to hold in tension the dualities of warfare and peacekeeping, blending martial prowess with empathy, cultural sensitivity, and collaborative problem-solving. These traits are key in a global context where military operations range from peacekeeping missions to disaster relief

---

[229] Hofheinz, "Indispensability of Virtues", 85; and Angelika Dörfler-Dierken, "Inner Leadership, or the Soldier's Responsibility for Humanity and Peace", in *Military and Character*, 39–48.
[230] Hofheinz, "Indispensability of Virtues", 87.

and support for democratic reform and governance. The emphasis on such virtues signals a departure from the traditional focus on military valor alone, and underlines the new duty of armed forces to cultivate moral soldier-citizens capable of navigating the ethical intricacies of their assignments. Such a transformation underscores the need for a code of conduct that accommodates the realities of contemporary conflicts, where strategic objectives intersect with humanitarian concerns.[231]

Swiss military historian and strategist Gustav Däniker argues that the soldier's role "is multifaceted, focusing not only on protection but also on helping and saving, aiming to make a significant contribution to peacekeeping and building a better world for all."[232] Soldiers are cosmopolitan guardians of the law, distinguished not just by their military expertise but by their legal, professional, and humanitarian competence. Military training programs today thus incorporate courses on international law, ethics, and the rules of engagement in an effort to prepare soldiers for the moral challenges they may face in diverse operational contexts. This holistic approach to military education ensures that courage, loyalty, and integrity are complemented by a profound understanding of human rights and a commitment to ethical decision-making.

Innere Führung

In the wake of World War II, Germany embarked on a critical reassessment of its military ethos, culminating in the development of the concept of *innere Führung* (inner leadership). *Innere Führung* was based on the view that "soldiers have rights as citizens of a democracy, and human dignity, freedom of religion, and freedom of conscience have to apply to them even during their military service."[233] This concept – striking in light of the horrible experience of German soldiers in two devastating world wars – is unique because "it is value-based and strengthens the virtue and responsibility of each soldier. It is the normative basis of personality development and the guideline for the training of military personnel."[234]

Innere Führung centers on two primary objectives: (1) to forge an ethical foundation for the military within a democratic framework, and (2) to empha-

---

[231] Ibid., 84–87.
[232] Gustav Däniker, *Wende Golfkrieg. Vom Wesen und Gebrauch künftiger Streitkräfte* (Frankfurt am Main: Report Verlag, 1992), 185–86.
[233] Stephen Pickard, introduction to *Military and Character*, 13–26, at 15, discussing Dörfler-Dierken, "Inner Leadership", 29–43.
[234] Pickard, introduction, 15.

size the accountability of military personnel for their actions.[235] This dual focus promotes a value system that guides professional behavior and soldiers' broader responsibilities as democratic citizens. Training extends beyond combat preparedness to include human rights education, ethical decision-making skills, and an appreciation for the moral complexities inherent in warfare. *Innere Führung* directs soldiers to remain combat-ready while stressing a commitment to the pursuit of justice, mercy, and peace. Leadership is characterized by mutual respect, ethical introspection, and collaborative decision-making. This approach enhances unit cohesion and guarantees that military actions align with societal expectations.[236]

The concept of *innere Führung* has generated the idea of soldiers as citizens in uniform, emphasizing their role in upholding democratic principles and human rights. It has helped to elevate soldiers from mere instruments of state power to virtuous and moral agents entrusted to maintain harmony even while discharging their military duties. Military personnel are encouraged to move beyond "unconditional obedience" and instead actively consider their orders and actions, since the "ultimate decision-making authority remains the conscience of each individual." This new ethic creates a strong connection between military service and the principles of democracy, motivating soldiers to demonstrate moral courage, advocate for justice, and align their military duties consistently with the democratic social principles they protect. A soldier's mission is fulfilled "when, out of inner conviction, they actively stand up for human dignity, freedom, peace, justice, equality, solidarity, and democracy as the guiding values of our state."[237]

The Reciprocal Influence of Military Virtues and Societal Values

The reciprocal influence between military virtues and societal values is a dynamic interplay that extends beyond mere tactical considerations. Concepts such as *miles protector* and *innere Führung* underscore the imperative for military conduct to be grounded in principles of justice, integrity, and ethical accountability and guided by underlying commitments to democracy, social order, and rule of law. By embracing such principles, the modern military in late liberal societies has slowly transformed itself from a mere defender of state interests and policies to a proactive guardian of democratic ideals and human rights. Beyond the battlefield, the influence of military virtues permeates into the fabric of society, shaping individual character and collective val-

---

[235] Cornelius-Bundschuh, "The Military Defense System", 29–30.
[236] Dörfler-Dierken, "Inner Leadership", 47–50.
[237] Cornelius-Bundschuh, "The Military Defense System", 29–30.

ues. Soldiers who embody virtues like discipline and honor during their service not only demonstrate their commitment to ethical conduct but also serve as exemplars within their communities after deployment. As German military scholar Hartwig von Schubert puts it:

> For a long time, armed conflicts within states – civil wars – have accounted for by far the largest share of warfare on earth. Therefore, strategic thinking in society must focus on much more than purely military capabilities. The decisive part in overcoming and pacifying conflicts must be played by "brave" civilian actors. Hardly anyone demands this more emphatically and passionately than soldiers returning from missions. The state and civil society should listen to them and, above all, learn this insight from them.[238]

The disciplined perspective cultivated in soldiers trained for contemporary conflicts can enrich the democratic dialogue within their communities. Their experiences can reinforce the rights and values that the military defends, fostering a culture of moral leadership and personal responsibility. This character formation within the military serves as a testament to its broader commitment to safeguarding national security and promoting a culture of virtue and integrity that transcends the battlefield, positively influencing the ethical landscape of society.

The Price of Serving: The Effects of Military Service and Challenges of Reintegration

Military service significantly impacts the physical and mental well-being of those who serve. Operating under high-stress conditions and maintaining a state of constant vigilance demand immense physical and psychological resilience. Many service members "suffer life-changing injuries, visible or otherwise, whilst serving their country."[239] These injuries result in a long and challenging journey, especially as they adapt to changed ways of life as civilians again.

> At the level of an individual combatant ... an ongoing threat of being killed in a war zone can generate in this person, including after the war, not simply occasional moments of fear but a sustained condition of fearfulness, which in turn can undermine

---

[238] Schubert, "Which Morals Society Should Learn from the Military", 77.
[239] Martin Elbe, "From the Playing Field to the Battlefield: Does Sport in the Military Promote the Formation of a Specific Character?" in *Military and Character*, 105-22, at 105.

the person's morally informed rational judgment and further undermine his or her autonomy and (relatedly) self-worth, thereby exacerbating the prior condition of fearfulness – and so on in a vicious circle of psychological decline and damage.[240]

Psychological and Moral Injuries

The physical wounds sustained in combat often force military personnel to undergo the long and arduous process of physical rehabilitation, frequently accompanied by a profound sense of loss. Equally debilitating are the psychological and moral wounds sustained during deployment. Psychological and moral injuries profoundly affect service members' ability to reintegrate into their pre-service life. Encountering extreme suffering, violence, and death during deployment changes their view of the world around them and makes everyday life and the concerns of their home country seem trivial. This dissonance can trigger "a creeping process of marginalization or alienation" as veterans struggle to reconcile their experiences with civilian life.[241]

Consequently, many veterans endure mental health struggles, such as post-traumatic stress disorder (PTSD), anxiety, depression, and moral injury, underscoring the lasting effects of their service experiences. PTSD – characterized by flashbacks, severe anxiety, and uncontrollable thoughts about traumatic events – arises from exposure to life-threatening situations inherent in military operations. Moral injury, a relatively new concept, stems from deep psychological distress caused by actions or inactions that violate a soldier's ethical beliefs, leading to enduring feelings of guilt, shame, and a crisis of identity. These "hidden wounds of war" highlight the psychological landscape soldiers must adapt to after deployment.[242]

Reintegration Challenges for Veterans and their Families

Transitioning from the structured and collective environment of military service to civilian life is often challenging for veterans. The camaraderie, purpose, and communal identity that define military life vastly differ from the realities of returning home. This change can cause disorientation, as the familiar routines

---

[240] Seumas Miller, "Moral Injury, Moral Character, and Military Combatants", in *Military and Character*, 141–52, at 148–49.

[241] Isolde Karle and Niklas Peuckmann, "In the Shadow of the Operation: Moral and Spiritual Injuries as New Challenges for Pastoral Care in the German Armed Forces", in *Military and Character*, 153–66, at 159–60.

[242] Ibid., 166.

and bonds formed in service are replaced by the individualistic and less regimented nature of civilian society.

The difficulties of military service and reintegration extend to the families of those who serve. Deployments create a unique set of challenges for military families, who must live with the absence of a loved one while maintaining day-to-day life. Children may experience academic and behavioral problems stemming from the weight of a parent's absence and the constant moves and adjustments required by the military lifestyle. Spouses bear the emotional and logistical burdens of managing their shifting households single-handedly amid constant worry about their partner's safety in conflict zones. In turn, soldiers also "sometimes miss biographically important events, such as the birth or enrollment of a child, a milestone birthday of a good friend, or the death and funeral of a close relative. Deployment is like a time bubble into which the soldiers are taken. They become part of a parallel world that has little in common with their other everyday world. As a result, experiences of distance come between the families and the soldiers."[243]

While eagerly anticipated, a soldier's return home can mark the beginning of a new set of hurdles as families adjust to having their loved ones back. Families must reacquaint themselves with changed individuals who may have experienced profound transformations in their worldview, temperament, and physical and mental health. As a result, family members may feel disconnected from their loved ones and wrestle with the inability to help them during this difficult time.

Public Perception

The shift from combat to civilian life presents significant obstacles for veterans as they try to reconcile their intense wartime experiences with the everyday norms of a society largely untouched by the direct impacts of conflict. The readjustment period is hindered by psychological wounds incurred during service, wounds that "are not visible and are therefore hardly noticed by society or the military."[244] This often results in the public's misunderstanding of veterans' experiences and mental health issues. Stereotypes and stigmas, particularly around conditions like PTSD and moral injury, obstruct returning soldiers' efforts to reintegrate, impacting their employment opportunities and their ability to engage in meaningful social interactions. On duty, "soldiers tend to be cherished as chivalrous heroes, or at least as 'our boys' (and girls)", but "returning personnel of warfare are often considered as a liability – suffering from PTSD,

---

[243] Ibid. 155–60.
[244] Ibid., 155.

suspected of indecent behavior while fighting, and asked by the general public to keep their wartime experience to themselves, especially when military intervention meets with societal and political criticism."[245] The public's focus on heroism can alienate those who return bearing emotional and psychological scars.

Despite fulfilling their duties abroad, returning veterans often find themselves at odds with the "publicly staged image of a brave or sacrificial fighter."[246] They often feel misunderstood and unable to identify with an idealized solider portrayal that does not reflect the complexities and traumas of their service. Media depictions, the nature of military engagements, and their outcomes significantly influence public attitudes. While the courage and sacrifices of military personnel are sometimes lauded, controversial military operations can provoke scrutiny and debate, negatively affecting how returning veterans are perceived.[247]

The dilemmas faced by soldiers and their subsequent actions in service sometimes clash with the prevailing values of the societies they return to. For example, the use of drones, asymmetric warfare, and the proportionality of military actions in response to threats requires soldiers and their leaders to make difficult decisions that, while legally and tactically justified, may not align with moral sentiments at home. Upon return home, German ethicist Torsten Meires writes, veterans "have to live under the general suspicion of having killed as well as having suffered without a plausible cause."[248] These shifting views and treatment of veterans underscore the dissonance between the idealized image of the soldier and the reality of their postservice lives, further complicating their progression toward reintegration and healing. Divergences between operational realities and public expectations fuel societal debate on the purpose and value of military engagements in contemporary conflicts. Some advocate for a more isolationist stance and question the rationale behind foreign interventions, while others emphasize the necessity of military engagement in safeguarding national security and promoting global stability.

Acknowledgment and Support

Addressing the impact of military service on servicemen and women requires a comprehensive approach that extends beyond mere acknowledgment to active support and integration efforts. Fulfilling this objective requires a concerted effort from the community, military organizations, health-care providers, the

---

[245] Meireis, "After Chivalry", 123–24.
[246] Karle and Peuckmann, "In the Shadow", 165.
[247] Schubert, "Which Morals Society Should Learn from the Military", 83–85.
[248] Meireis, "After Chivalry", 132.

church, and policymakers. Effective reintegration strategies should include vocational training, employment assistance, and access to mental health services tailored to the unique challenges that returning service members face.[249]

Community-based programs, peer support networks, and health-care services can facilitate a smoother transition for veterans and their families. To improve the adaptation process for all family members before, during, and after deployment, educational assistance for children and family counseling should be offered. Programs designed to help families understand the psychological impacts of deployment and combat exposure can create a more supportive home environment for returning veterans.[250]

Commemorative practices shape public perceptions and promote a sense of shared history and values. Memorial services, Veterans Day celebrations, and monument dedications honor military personnel and provide spaces for reflection, mourning, and celebration. However, these practices need to evolve beyond simply celebrating heroism and traditional notions of bravery and must also acknowledge the hardships of military service more accurately. By doing so, these practices can contribute to a more nuanced understanding of military personnel are appropriately and respectfully remembered by society and assist them in transitioning to civilian life.

The Role of the Church in Military Ethics and Peacebuilding

The church provides a critical perspective that prompts the military and society to consider the deeper implications of warfare and peace. Its role is not limited to providing abstract theological discourse but extends to practical involvement in military ethics, peacebuilding, and the care of veterans and their families. The church's fidelity to peace and human dignity offers a counterpoint to the narratives of militarism and violence, encouraging military leaders and state policymakers to consider the long-term consequences of their decisions.[251] Religious leaders contribute to shaping a moral framework that emphasizes the sanctity of life, the importance of justice, and the pursuit of harmony through preaching, pastoral care, and participation in ethical debates.

---

[249] Ibid.
[250] Karle and Peuckmann, "In the Shadow", 155–58, 164–66.
[251] Cornelius-Bundschuh, "The Military Defense System", 29–34; Dörfler-Dierken, "Inner Leadership", 45–47; and Schubert, "Which Morals Society Should Learn", 87–92.

Spiritual Care

The church plays a crucial role in guiding ethical considerations around war and providing support to veterans and their families. Military chaplains serve as spiritual guides and confidential counselors, equipped to care for the psychological and moral injuries that underlie the hidden wounds of war, providing a source of solace and guidance for those grappling with existential questions that frequently arise from combat experiences. Chaplains' expertise helps service members overcome trauma by guiding them through processes of recovery, forgiveness, and healing that align with their individual beliefs, confronting the moral and spiritual conflicts of service. Military chaplains also work to support the families of servicemen and women, acknowledging the ripple effects of deployment-related trauma on loved ones. Family counseling and support groups offer a platform for spouses, children, and other family members to share their experiences, concerns, and coping strategies.[252]

Pastoral care services and military chaplaincy offer specialized support to servicemen and women dealing with the aftermath of deployment-related trauma. They provide a comprehensive care system that tackles the spiritual, emotional, and psychological dimensions of recovery. This care is essential in assisting individuals to heal from the visible and invisible wounds of war, including their physical injuries, PTSD, and moral injuries. Military chaplaincy initiatives exemplify the church's response to the aftermath of deployment. These programs are designed to facilitate personal reflection and community building, creating a sense of belonging and mutual understanding among participants. They also play an essential role in bridging the gap between the military and civilian realms by providing a multiprofessional support system for veterans struggling with the challenges of reintegration. Through these initiatives, the church offers spiritual and emotional support, affirming the importance of faith and community in the healing process and ensuring that servicemen and women find a path to recovery within a supportive and understanding social system.[253]

Christian Advocacy

As an institution rooted in spiritual guidance and ethical teaching, the church has historically served as a compass for navigating the moral dilemmas posed by warfare and peacebuilding efforts. Through its teachings, provision of pastoral care, and advocacy for peace, the church urges the military institu-

---

[252] Karle and Peuckmann, "In the Shadow", 161–64.
[253] Ibid.

tion and society to consider the implications of warfare and strive for a world where disputes are resolved through dialogue and reconciliation. In turn, the church can address the intricacies of modern conflicts while supporting the healing and integration of veterans and their families into a society that prioritizes peace, justice, and human dignity.[254]

As a moral authority, the church has a responsibility to advocate for policies and practices that align with Christian ethics, the needs of veterans and their families, and peacebuilding initiatives aimed at resolving conflicts without violence. The church is uniquely positioned to remind the public of the personal sacrifices made by military personnel and the complexities of decision-making in combat zones. By highlighting the human dimensions of military operations, the church can foster empathy and understanding among the civilian population, closing the divide in perception and promoting a communal spirit of support and gratitude.

Concluding Reflections

The military's role has been transformed in the evolving landscape of the twenty-first century. Leading German statesman Thomas Bagger observes that "global crises and conflicts concern us, not just because they disturb our normative perceptions of the world, but because many of these directly affect our security, our prosperity, and the future of our democracy."[255] Pursuing peace, particularly amid asymmetric threats and unconventional warfare, requires a thoughtful, coordinated approach to conflict resolution. Defense policies have increasingly emphasized collaboration with international allies through joint operations, signifying a strategic shift toward a more interconnected and mutually supportive global defense. The military now engages not only in defense but also in peacekeeping, humanitarian aid, and efforts to stabilize regions. This broader engagement emphasizes nonviolent resolutions and prioritizes civilian well-being, contributing to a more equitable and peaceful global community.

Advanced technologies, such as cyber capabilities and unmanned aerial vehicles, have revolutionized military strategies while also posing new ethical dilemmas. These innovations challenge traditional notions of accountability and sovereignty, blurring the lines between combat and humanitarian aid. Military personnel now assume roles beyond the warrior archetype, encompassing di-

---

[254] Cornelius-Bundschuh, "The Military Defense System", 29–30; Hofheinz, "Indispensability of Virtues."; Karle and Peuckmann, "In the Shadow", 166.

[255] Thomas Bagger, "Germany, We Need to Talk", *Internationale Politik Quarterly* 3 (2021), https://ip-quarterly.com/en/germany-we-need-talk, quoted with discussion in Schubert, "Which Morals Should Society Learn", 74–75n16.

plomacy, nation building, and humanitarian relief efforts, necessitating a nuanced understanding of ethical obligations.

The military must adapt with reflective approaches as global conflicts grow increasingly complex and interconnected. This entails evolving strategic and technological capabilities while maintaining unwavering adherence to ethical principles. The concept of the *miles protector* symbolizes the soldier's dual role as a defender of peace and societal values. Moral considerations are integral to military operations, exemplified by concepts like *innere Führung*, which embeds democratic principles and human rights within the military ethos. Legal frameworks establish a foundation for ethical conduct, but ethical engagement requires surpassing legal compliance to consider wider implications for human dignity and societal values.

As one of society's most venerable institutions – and one that is essential for a society's survival in the modern world of warfare and terrorism – the military stands not only as a guardian of national security but also as a formidable crucible for character development, instilling virtues of courage, discipline, loyalty, and a profound sense of duty in its members. These virtues, deeply embedded in military culture, offer a blueprint for ethical conduct that extends beyond the confines of service, influencing broader societal norms and values.

The future of military service hinges on its adaptability to evolving geopolitical landscapes while remaining anchored in ethical and value-based principles that bind it to society. Through sustained support and understanding of the military's role and sacrifices, society can strengthen this crucial connection, ensuring that both the armed forces and civilians progress together toward shared goals. Continuous education, open dialogue, and interdisciplinary research are essential for effectively responding to ethical complexities. By fostering a culture of ethical reflection and collaboration, the military can develop strategies that meet operational needs while upholding societal moral values.

Ongoing dialogue among military leaders, the church, and society is vital for shaping approaches to peace and conflict that align with contemporary moral imperatives. Ethical considerations, historical insights, and the transformative potential of peacebuilding efforts are key to addressing the challenges of modern warfare and realizing a vision of a just and peaceful world.

Concluding Reflections: Enduring Issues, New Challenges

This volume is intended as a summation of a six-year, ten volume project on the impact of modern social institutions on character formation and ethical education in late modern pluralistic societies. The project, and this concluding volume, have analyzed the shifting roles and impacts of both traditional social spheres of family, religion, law, politics, and markets, and the comparatively newer social spheres of education, academic research, health care, the media, and the military.

All ten of these social systems, we have argued, remain essential for building a good life and a good society in late modern pluralistic societies today. Every advanced society, including liberal societies, has family systems of love and procreation, religious systems of ritual and doctrine, political systems of authority and liberty, legal systems of justice and order, economic systems of trade and property, media systems of communication and dissemination of news and information, and educational systems of preservation, application, and creation of knowledge and scientific advance. Many advanced societies, particularly in Western liberal societies, also have massive systems of science, technology, health care, and military power with vast influence over and through all of the other social systems. These pervasive social systems lie at the foundation of modern advanced societies, and they anchor the vast pluralities of associations and social interactions that might happen to exist at any given time.

Each of these social spheres, furthermore, has internal value systems, institutionalized rationalities, and normative customs and expectations that together help to shape each individual's morality and character. Each of these social spheres, moreover, has its own professionals and experts who shape and implement its internal structures and processes. The normative network created by these social spheres, however, has become ever more interwoven, shifting, and fragile, especially since traditional social systems, such as religion and the family, have eroded in their durability and power, while other social systems, such as science, health care, the market, military, and media, have become more powerful. Even so, we submit that each social sphere deserves a place in late modern pluralistic societies, and no social system should be allowed to monopolize private and public morality and ethical education.

In the foregoing chapters, we have identified several core normative functions, promising pathways, and troubling developments for these ten spheres separately and together to foster greater justice, freedom, benevolence, and peace at home and abroad. In drawing this volume to a close, we present here brief summaries of the ten chapters and suggest some implications for further investigation and study.

The Family

The family is humanity's oldest social institution that ideally is characterized by love, care, and hope. It has long been regarded as the cornerstone of social organization and character formation. But today it is sometimes questioned as outdated or even oppressive, especially for women and children. As an institution, the family is closely interwoven with other social institutions, including schools, work, public administration, consumption, leisure, and legal, political, and religious regulations. All of these shape the way we get married, raise and educate children, transmit property and wealth, teach and exemplify values and ethics, and form and dissolve family bonds. In what ways are these multi-institutional and multisystemic connections helpful, and where do they become unfruitful or even threatening? That is a central question raised by our project.

It was not only for our ancestors that the family could be a place of tyranny and abuse, poverty and deprivation, waste and neglect, from which there was little escape. Abuse and exploitation in marriage continue to cause massive and lasting damage to many women and children. Domestic violence remains a problem, albeit slowed by women's rights movements, tough criminal justice measures, and remarkable new self-help movements. Similarly, children suffer the effects of physical, emotional, and verbal abuse and inadequate education and health care. Devastating violence against children has continued at an alarming rate in modern liberal societies.

Even so, modern families remain for many an indispensable forum for character formation and ethical education, and modern liberal societies feature numerous valuable interrelationships between the social systems of family, education, law, politics, religion, communication, and health care. Some of these new institutional interrelationships have shored up the family's traditional role in moral character formation and ethical education. But others have been threatening, particularly the dominance of media and market-driven communication in childhood, adolescence, and family life. So, too, have been the demands of the modern economy that have separated work from home and parents from children, as well as the regulations of the state that now govern the inner workings of the family – providing care and support, punishing abuse and neglect, and fostering health and education.

Several liberal scholars have encouraged modern societies to abandon or abolish the institution of the marital family and leave questions of sexuality, childbearing, and child care entirely to the unhindered and unstructured free choice of the individual. This is dangerous, we argue. After all, it was precisely the dangers and violence of the sexual state of nature that forced men and women to form organized societies with their various marital, political, religious, and other voluntary institutions. The family is by no means perfect, but it is vital for character formation and ethical education from infancy through adulthood. When it functions properly, the family remains society's best institution to find enduring love, mutual care, wealth production, and physical and mental health.

Religion

Religion is outdated, and religious institutions are in irreversible decline. This opinion can be found in many quarters of the liberal West today. From a global perspective, however, it is highly debatable: international statistics on people's religious affiliation, we saw, indicate that the percentage of people worldwide who professed some form of religion rose from 80.8 percent in 1970 to 87 percent in 2000, and the number continues to grow. It is true, however, that in contrast to the global persistence of religions, many liberal societies in North America, Europe, Australia, and parts of Asia and Africa – especially in economically and scientifically influential countries – have witnessed the dwindling appeal and resonance of religious institutions, while the market, media, medicine, and parts of the scientific research industry have grown in power and impact.

Strong pockets of old and new religions remain in place in many liberal societies, often using new technologies and communication methods to build their communities. And migration has brought more religious believers and institutions. But a number of monohierarchical, patriarchal, and gerontocratic relationships in religion, politics, and families have also emerged prominently, particularly with the recent shift from liberal democratic conditions to autocratic forms in various countries – accompanied by the suppression of free media and the influence of authoritarian or even dictatorial politics on the legal system, religion, and science. And that has raised the hard questions: Why is it so difficult today to demonstrate and prove the effectiveness of religion as the foundation of a free society? Why do religion and faith so often go hand in hand with developments that hinder or even prevent the pursuit of freedom, truth, and justice?

One answer to this question, we argue, lies in the widespread forms of liberal piety and weak theology that have led especially to the traditional church's dwindling popularity in the West. This liberal piety does not imbue a robust sense of the creativity and richness of God, of God's spirit and the divine powers that sustain, save, judge, ennoble, and exalt people. Instead, it focuses more narrowly on spiritualism and on a human religious spirit, understood in an individualistic and rational way, and on a numinous transcendence or empty images and feelings of God. A biblically oriented knowledge of the divine spirit, we submit, can protect us from such empty and implausible concepts of God, and such vague talk of God's abstract omnipotence. In contrast, the divine spirit of justice, freedom, truth, peace, philanthropy, and love of neighbor is a true powerhouse of goodness. It works in the complicated real world in many forms and institutions, not only in religion.

Another answer, William Schweiker argues, lies in the weakness of much religious and moral communication in pluralistic societies. Instead of assuming that such forms of communication are inherently good, he argues that theology and theological ethics must engage critically and constructively with reality, with truth-seeking, and with deploying and demonstrating the power of specific religious concepts and practices of value and morality. The tradition of virtue ethics has played a major role in this effort, connecting entire networks of values to each other and to daily life. Although virtue ethics often propagates the isomorphism of the character and soul of the individual and the social community, a robust new form of "Christian humanism" that draws on the tradition of virtue can help resist totalitarian orientations and confront metadiscourses and metanarratives.

Another answer lies in international ecumenical theology, Friederike Nüssel argues. This has been especially good in promoting values of justice, peace, human rights, and the protection of natural environments. Further answers lie in recognizing the constructive role of religion in moral, legal, political, and economic developments and reforms in different parts of the world, particularly during times of political and economic transition.

Even so, it is important to note several critical questions about the role of religion in modern "pluralistic" societies. Jennifer Herdt, for example, argues that Max Weber's multisystemic social theory has been heuristically enlightening, but it sometimes overlooks the formative significance of polyindividual plurality and religious emotionality in late modern societies. Admiel Kosman, too, lifts up the weighty traditions of personalism in both Judaism and Christianity – perhaps best exemplified by religiously and ethically focused I-Thou thinking – that push against the power of institutional religious systems. Certain traditions of family ritual and piety, especially in Asian societies still influenced by Confucianism, sometimes find themselves in tension with today's global economic, political, and scientific developments.

Perhaps the most critical question, raised by Philipp Stoellger, is whether a focus on religious and other institutions in modern pluralistic societies contains a latent "will to power" – that is, an attempt to understand social systems more fully in order to use them more effectively to certain (pernicious) ends. Our hope is that, on the contrary, what will shine forth from all our project volumes, and from other such interdisciplinary studies of late modern pluralistic societies, is a strong ethos of endeavoring to protect the weak and disadvantaged and an ethos of developing and improving forms of justice and freedom in intrinsic connection with religiosity, not only with Christianity.

Politics

In late modern pluralistic societies, the state is a powerful institution for moral character formation, ethical education, and the communication of values. State officials themselves may or may not be effective moral models to emulate; that is as true today as it was in the past, despite all the discourses on the moral character of the good ruler. But the late modern state and its legal and bureaucratic systems affect and effect moral formation in a number of ways. It does so through its many "thou shalt" commands ("pay your taxes"; "educate your children"; "register your properties") and "thou shalt not" commands ("do not kill", "do not steal", "do not bear false witness"). It does so through its formal state-run systems of education from kindergarten to university, and its less formal but pervasive instructions about private and public health, safety, and welfare. It does so through its networks of regulations of markets, military life, health care, and more. It does so through the teachings, practices, symbols, ceremonies, and statuary of state-established or state-supported churches, schools, and charities.

The state's moral education also comes through the myriad ways that state policies and procedures nudge, encourage, incentivize, and facilitate citizens to adopt certain behaviors and avoid others. Tax deductions encourage marriage, charity, and home ownership. Heavy license fees and taxes discourage smoking and drinking. Zoning, land use, and nuisance laws guide the appropriate uses of properties. Environmental laws demand attention to duties of stewardship. Civil rights laws encourage more inclusive employment decisions and public accommodations. Same-sex marriage rights invite a more expansive understanding of domestic relations. Education licenses define the baseline content of public and private schools. Rather like trees and plants bending to the light, both individuals and nonstate institutions often position and incline their moral choices and habits to enjoy the benefits of state policies – and sometimes contort or camouflage themselves to avoid the political shadows.

Many people in the liberal and democratic societies of the West, however, are perplexed by the increasingly autocratic and even dictatorial conditions that are emerging in societies for which freedom, truth, and justice were high values not so long ago. Ideally, the core purpose of politics is to enable the governance of a particular people and territory and to win the loyalty of citizens in the process. But what happens when the state becomes a tyrant? These questions continue to make headlines today, not only in late modern liberal societies but in other forms of society, such as Ukraine, Hong Kong, Iran, North Korea, the Philippines, and countries in North Africa or Latin America facing rogue and oppressive regimes or invading foreign powers.

When political encroachments on freedom, morality, and conscience are minor, as is the case today in most late modern pluralistic societies, citizens generally have legal, political, and media means at their disposal to defend themselves. They can seek an injunction, file a lawsuit, lobby for a change in the law, file petitions and complaints, mobilize shame through exposure in the media, disobey or demonstrate, as we have seen, for example, in recent campaigns in the United States against gross racism and police violence. But when political encroachments on freedom and an ethos of truth and justice are more severe, as they are in many parts of the world, oppressed citizens may resort to harsher measures. If they have no legal recourse, they may resist those who violate their faith, freedom, family, and other fundamental rights – if necessary, with violence and then often with threatening consequences. The new millennium has brought with it enormous new challenges that raise these questions anew and test and the remits and limits of fundamental political systems internally and externally. It is therefore essential for modern pluralistic societies and states to address their own challenges and strengthen the role of all social systems, institutions, and citizens in the pursuit of freedom, justice, truth, peace, well-being, and shared humanity.

Law

Our focus on the legal sphere has illuminated the fruitful tensions between the state's positive laws and the many other normative systems at work in complex structures of late modern societies. Law consists, in the broadest sense, of all written and unwritten norms that regulate human behavior: moral precepts, family rules, church regulations, state laws, trade laws, regional customs, local conventions, and others. All of these written and practiced rules help to shape the morality and character of people and nations by encouraging and guiding their choices, behavior, relationships, and institutions by prescribing and prohibiting, supporting and facilitating, rewarding and punishing, restricting and influencing.

In premodern societies, these different laws overlapped, as they were often enacted and enforced by interwoven religious, political, economic, feudal, and familial authorities. In modern liberal societies, however, the state is a differentiated sphere of action, and its legal system is formally separated from the internal laws of nonstate associations. But it is important to realize that all the internal regulations and orders of nonstate associations are still critical sources for the moral formation and ethical education of individuals and groups today, particularly the formative power that emanates from parents and people in the education and health-care systems, in the market and media, and in other social systems and institutions, and the valuable ethos of self-help and personal commitment.

State laws do set and, if necessary, enforce a base line of civil morality that every liberal society needs. Criminal laws and the public prosecution of offenders communicated through the media and education systems, as well as successful processes of resocialization, have a considerable impact on general character development, ethical education, and communication of values – even in late modern pluralistic societies. The state works through broad networks of regulatory laws and behavioral suggestions, often latently. Constitutional laws and human rights documents are impressively enforced both nationally and internationally. There has been talk of a "civil religion" by Robert Bellah and others and a "constitutional patriotism" by Jürgen Habermas to be cultivated with enthusiasm, but also with concerns about moral and moralistic overrides without quality control of value systems.

It remains indispensable for the proper rule of law in late modern societies to foster and feature the separation of powers and the reciprocal critical and self-critical control of state law and political education, family ethos, religious values, and professional ethics in education, health care, and academic research. It has also proved critical to enumerate and vindicate constitutionally enshrined rights for individuals and groups. Important, too, is the exemplary function of judges, lawyers, and others who represent the development of the law as paradigmatically leading citizens. Precisely because they are not as subject to the changing political demands for compromises and the constant procurement of new loyalties as those with political and media influence, these legal professionals can contribute significantly to the cultivation of a fruitful ethos of social order, rule of law, protection of rights, and the pursuit of justice.

Health Care

In many respects, health care and medicine today can be seen as prime loci for character development, ethical education, and communication of values in late modern pluralistic societies. Health care, in conjunction with rapid scientific and medical technological development, serves to protect the suffering and the weak, offering help and comfort not only to those affected by illness but also to their relatives and friends. It therefore meets the highest standards of humanitarian ethics.

But Eva Winkler and many of her medical colleagues ask: How can the quality of medical treatment and trust in the medical profession be maintained if economic and political warnings about overly expensive interventions and therapies constantly accompany the work? How should doctors behave toward medically promising but highly costly developments in the pharmaceutical industry and medical technology? Can and should medical professionals try to prevent the economic profit interests of investors from deforming an essentially egalitarian health-care system in a class-based society?

Günter Thomas shows how "care" for the sick has long been thought of in the context of a person-to-person relationship, rather than in institutional terms. Today, this approach to caring for the sick should remain relevant in the value system of health-care organizations – not just medical institutions but also insurance systems, the public and political support for health care, the ethos of doctors, the nursing staff in clinics, and the very different expectations of the patients and their relatives. How can this complex network of different value systems, orientations, and expectations be brought into view in a meaningful way?

At minimum, everyone involved professionally in health-care institutions should be expected to have the competence to deal carefully with different ethical perspectives and convictions, not only among patients but also among clinical staff. Included in this scenario is the highly valuable ethical goal of giving the patient a voice, especially when conflicts arise between the caring professionals and the patient (or the patient's relatives and friends, in situations where the patient cannot truly articulate his or her own will).

The history of nursing can help shed light on the ways in which the culture and ethos of care have changed over time, and can perhaps suggest further changes. Initially supported by religious and moral foundations of a recognized ethic of devotion to the sick and poor and an associated sense of dignity, nursing addressed not only physical and material needs but also mental and spiritual needs. Over time, as religious components were steadily reduced and medical ones more strongly emphasized, the competencies and leadership roles of nurses were subordinated to the authority of doctors.

Similarly, great scientific and medical technological developments of recent decades and the increasingly efficient provision of medical and therapeutic care have consolidated the reputation and power of medicine and health care within the network of social systems. However, the inflationary costs of these positive developments and the heightened expectations associated with medical performance have increased the social, political, and economic pressure on those working in medicine and health care. This pressure sometimes leads to mistakes, attrition, and burnout.

Recognizing such pitfalls in the health-care system helps us to see in other areas of society the negative impact that comes from neglecting the financial remuneration and appreciation of people in supportive roles. Future tasks in the area of character development and ethical education should include examining ways to increase financial rewards and personal appreciation of medical help and care, but also realistically addressing quality of life and personal freedom of the sick.

Academic Research

The combination of research and teaching in the same institution is a valuable contribution to character formation and ethical education. The participation of students from different scientific disciplines and from different countries in the academic enterprise is an advantage both to them and to their teachers. A global community that is committed to the concentrated search for knowledge and truth and that has developed many forms of critical examination of all truth claims is an excellent medium for character development, ethical education, and communication of values in all societies of the world.

However, this breadth of international and multidisciplinary communication and academic research today also entails dangers. In addition to the disciplinarily controlled scientific search for truth, ethical concerns can bring strong political and ideological expectations and conflicts far removed from academic work into university communication processes. The National Socialist contamination of German universities after 1933 is a particularly frightening example of this. But even today (in 2024), extreme political and military conflicts can have devastating effects on the intellectual climate and their institutions, even at highly respected research universities such as Harvard.

William Schweiker describes the classic ideas that led to the founding of research universities in the West, including a religious or moral horizon of investigation, the idea of the unity of human reason, and the belief in the possibility of character formation through academic training. Today's university has moved a long way away from these original guiding ideas. The typical university today is a collection of different disciplines, each with its own methods, purposes, and scientific norms, leading to intellectual silos that largely forgo communication with other silos. However, some fruitful counterdevelopments include the multidisciplinary programs, not least exemplified in the interdisciplinary project distilled in this volume.

Andreas Glaeser has formulated the decisive challenge, however: What constitutes a good institution, particularly a good academic research institution?

Classical references to transcendent entities, such as God, are no more helpful here than naturalistic scientism or a well-intentioned romanticism of nature, Glaeser argues. Rather, the range of tasks exemplified by our series of consultations and publications in this project may illustrate a way forward. This kind of academic research and interdisciplinary scientific collaboration avoids metaphysical searches for orientation, but also steers clear of appeals to "pure logic" or "pure faith" as the last bastions of an "absolute truth." On the other hand, academic work itself may not be the optimal source for moral guidance. As many academics can attest, the academy is not always a place that fosters knowledge about how to live well and how to live fruitfully in community.

Nevertheless, while moral communication often manifests ambivalences and ambiguities, it is possible to distinguish among different calibers of truth-seeking and to speak of a multimodal "spirit of truth" in the academy as well as in life. For many people, the hope for certainty is a guiding star in their search for truth. In education and science, however, proposals of certainty are always subjected to critical scrutiny. While consensus is highly valued in moral issues, and consensus theories of truth are sought, in science and education the fleeting nature of consensus, long-established common errors, and seductive or even enforced social consensus are recognized as problems. More sophisticated forms of knowledge of truth besides certainty and consensus are recommended and further developed under the norms of consistency, coherence, factual correctness, and empirical and historical verifiability and rationality.

Universities and their disciplinary manifestations have a variety of potential orientations that can correct, improve, and refine the individual's experience of life and the world. The correction of individual as well as culturally and academically established perspectives on the world and life is particularly important in situations of political and media manipulation and oppression. The devastating rise of "fake news" spread during Donald Trump's 2016 election campaign and presidential administration, for example, has renewed attention to the ethical appreciation of truth and the common search for truth. Suppression of free media and manipulation of legal systems in autocratic regimes are also reasons to value the truth.

One bulwark against efforts to suppress truth, freedom, and justice, we submit, is a global network of research universities and research institutions that are committed to the search for truth and the unmasking of false claims – even if these diverse efforts do not share a single voice or simple message. Examples of such efforts abound. In the natural sciences, for instance, many developments raise ethical questions because of problematic economic transformations triggered by technological innovations, or unintended consequences of discoveries. The enormous achievements in biomedical research over the past hundred years have benefited many areas of human life but have not eliminated "health gaps" between wealthy and poor countries. Institutions increasingly adopt guiding principle to prevent scientific misconduct and promote integrity in research and publications.

Many institutions also take self-critical initiatives to understand their complex histories. Here the humanities can play a significant role. For instance, a number of U.S. universities have delved into the history of their relationship with the legacy of slavery and taken corrective measures. Doing so, they demonstrate the power of historical and academic work for social, cultural, political, religious, and legal transformation. The interdisciplinary study of law and religion, too, has gained great momentum in recent decades, fueled by social, cultural, political, religious and legal transformations. In one sense the growth of this field marks a return to two of the disciplines that were at the center of the first universities in Western Europe. Biblical scholars, too, have drawn insightful lessons from the Hebrew Bible and the New Testament for how we learn to make sound moral judgments today and learn the ethical value of attending to and gaining new perspectives from the other. Moreover, as students in many different disciplines working in research settings strive to understand the value of their work for the common good, they can develop a deepened practical wisdom that goes beyond mere professional ethics toward real education in what it means to be a virtuous person. Our project thus has demonstrated that academic research in the humanities as well as the natural sciences has much to contribute to character formation and the transmission of values.

Education

Primary and secondary schools are obvious and critical sites for the development of character, ethical education, and the communication of values. From prekindergarten to twelfth grade, students learn not only essential information, skills, methods, and insights, but also gain a growing awareness of their place in the world, and the vocation where to apply their emerging talents. This early formative period of character formation and ethical education focuses on the promotion of personal and community integrity and the organization of educational processes. Ideally, this formal educational experience in schools stands alongside moral formation at home, spiritual catechesis in church, and practical learning and skill formation on the playground, in neighborhood gatherings, social clubs, and other sites of interaction.

In our day of political divisiveness and culture wars, however, basic education is especially fraught with landmines and potential pitfalls. Battles over revisionist histories, more inclusive literature, more expansive sexual education, and the promotion of either progressive or reactionary conservative values have threatened to rend many educational systems asunder. So, too, has been competition for resources and attention between public, state-run schools, and private, sometimes religious schools and their curricula, funding, admissions policies, and more. Politicians, philanthropists, media barons, foreign investors, and others have all contributed to these culture wars in schools. While acknowledging that there may be no consensus or easy solutions our project has outlined some of the dangers of politicizing education and has underscored the need for close examination of educational performance and results.

Some lessons can be gained from ancient texts and historical contexts, we have shown. The ancients had much to say about education as training of socially positive wishes and desires in an environment of differing ideological perspectives and moral attitudes. Early modern Protestant reformers, too, created the new public schools as "civic seminaries" designed to inculcate both religion and morality but also erudition and practical training to serve the commonweal. National contexts like the democratization of Germany after 1945, the reduction of bias against Aboriginal populations in early childhood education in Australia, and the introduction of meritocracy as a balance to traditional family values in South Korea all suggest both the promise and the power of principled redirection of a society through education.

Echoing the hopefulness of such developments, some of our contributors have advocated for greater commitment to proven methods for values education, drawing from various religious, legal, historical, and political sources. "Classical schools" and religious schools are back in vogue in many countries, and morally infused curricula are now on offer in growing numbers of public state schools as well as private schools. The common modern stress on education as a means of professional development or economic advancement can easily incorporate more attention to the fundamental question of a student's vocation, or calling, which itself is a question about the character with which one will live in the world. The practical and ethical orientation of education for vocation serves the development of a complex self-awareness as well as a cosmopolitan openness to the world and to the future. Literature, too, opens students in this way by presenting and asking questions about political, moral, and aesthetic ideas in environments both familiar and strange. Literature and various other media thus draw the student beyond a fixation on the current *Zeitgeist* and present problems, opening a world of moral imagination, ethical imitation, and cultural adaptation that help school young hearts and minds and prepare them for better decision-making as adults.

The Market

Markets are fundamental institutions of human society that provide essential (and also surplus) goods, services, and opportunities. Without markets, Jürgen von Hagen makes clear, human life would be reduced to an endless daily and dangerous hunt for and gathering of the minimum necessary for survival. This is, sadly, the condition from which poor and needy members of even wealthy societies continue to suffer, not to mention the many millions who today are ravaged by war, famine, and other natural or human tragedies, or live in refugee camps or in corrupt or broken states around the world. Yet in the pluralistic, liberal societies of late modernity, stable markets are designed to ensure that most people at least get the essentials to live – with private charity, diaconal support, and state welfare systems ideally supporting those who have too little.

Churches in the past, states and industry regulators in the present provide basic guidelines to ensure that markets function efficiently and that market participants keep their promises and refrain from blatantly immoral behavior and trading. In this sense, markets provide a foundation for a minimum level of economic morality and a platform for exposing fraudsters and criminals. Moreover, when they are open and fair, markets provide endless opportunities for people to share the fruits of their honest labor and to acquire and distribute the goods and services they need to support their loved ones and fellow human beings. Markets are not overseers and shapers of morality; that is left to the market participants themselves and the other social institutions (including families and churches) of which they are a part. But markets offer individuals and institutions the freedom and opportunity to express their moral choices and ethical preferences through buying and selling, advertising and advocating, and donating and distributing goods, services, ideas, and information.

Many economists today consider markets themselves to be amoral. But many of these economists take a moralistic view of the rational *homo economicus*, who strives to make the most efficient and effective decisions to maximize profits. This anthropology, which is incessantly taught to students of economics, has extended to many areas of life beyond the market, including decisions about faith, family, health care, education, research, the media, military decisions, and much more. Piet Naudé, Stephen Pickard, and critics from various fields, notably theology, ethics, sociology, and public policy, have pushed back against this grim caricature of the *homo economicus* of human nature. They have called for a robust return to norms of moral formation and forms of ethical calculation that take seriously the virtues and values of faith, hope, and love, as well as justice, mercy, and peace. It is these virtues and values that ultimately make our human life worth living, including our economic life.

Media

Our project has studied the mass media, including the printed press, radio and television, the film industry, and, more recently, the internet and social platforms. These new forms of communication – developed over the past century and expanded rapidly in the past three decades – have been the most revolutionary shift in communication since the creation of the printing press and the vernacularization of literature a half millennium ago. On one hand, these new media have dramatically democratized knowledge, or at least information sharing. On the other hand, the communication of values through these media sets in motion selective processes that privilege a limited set of values and create ethical prejudices and biases. This in turn has an impact on character development in large parts of the population. Five hundred years ago in the West, most forms of knowledge were captured in Latin texts, largely controlled by church and state authorities and their censors and licensors, and accessible only to the few who were educated. Today modern pluralistic societies are "media societies", where mass communication is omnipresent, and almost everyone has access to vast quantities of information. Ironically, however, new media giants still control the information, with both new forms of censorship and manipulation quietly still in place.

Mass media have particular importance for the communication of values in modern pluralistic societies. Strong interdependencies between media and the economy shape culture in countless ways and thus influence how ethical values are perpetuated or changed. The decisive role of mass media in arousing and attracting attention is both boon and bane, making possible the focus of activism against injustice and repression, but also providing forums for disinformation and propaganda. The highest qualities of human community – empathy, curiosity, compassion, good will – are often undermined by anonymous social media. Modern liberal societies have yet to develop a media-critical ethic that addresses these cultural challenges.

Media communication processes not only permeate the organization of other social spheres in late modern societies; they also exert enormous influence on everyday life and private spheres. The associated complexity and confusion pose a major challenge for individual orientation and social processes. Also challenging are the struggles to gain and maintain attention in media societies. Organized sport, politics, religion, civil society, business, science, education, and many other areas constantly compete for personal and public attention. Many dreams of achieving social harmony and understanding are linked to this fixation on getting attention – increasing one's followers and thus purportedly one's influence. Unfortunately, however, generating media attention can also deepen conflicts, provoke hatred, consolidate self-isolation in communication bubbles, and serve to spread fake news. The possibilities of controlling and manipulating human thought, feeling, and behavior are frightening. All attempts to counteract these possibilities through intensive moral communication alone remain inadequate.

Nicholas Couldry uses the term "datafied media" to warn that most human activities on the internet are only permitted – with or without the knowledge and consent of the actors (!) – because they can be registered and traced. They are registered as data that has potential economic value for the entities interested in them. Couldry is very concerned about the loss of high qualities of humanity and ethos, a loss that he associates with a disruption of "communicative symmetry." Communicative symmetry is essentially guaranteed in person-to-person communication. If it is missing, connections to the good driving forces of history and tradition are jeopardized, and an immense loss of human control of individual and communal developments becomes imminent. Although he warns against hasty negative reactions to this development, he sees an urgent need to develop a media-critical ethic that addresses these cultural challenges.

Günter Thomas, however, warns against the impression that people today are merely helpless observers of this complex media power. He encourages a double hermeneutic process in which people see themselves as responsible controllers and ask critically and self-critically about their own value preferences: What ideas of a good, just, and fruitful life determine our thoughts and actions? And further, what ideas of a good, just, and fruitful life are the most effective development trends in media practices? We should critically and self-critically examine the extent to which these value processes can mutually strengthen or weaken and block each other.

The Military

The role of the military has changed significantly since World War II, and new, disruptive developments of the twenty-first century have accelerated these changes. The pursuit of peace, especially in the midst of asymmetric threats and unconventional warfare, requires a thoughtful, coordinated approach to conflict resolution. Defense policy increasingly emphasizes cooperation with international allies through joint operations, signifying a strategic shift toward a more interconnected and mutually supportive global defense. The military is now engaged not only in national defense but also in peacekeeping, humanitarian aid, and regional stabilization efforts. This broader engagement emphasizes nonviolent solutions, prioritizes the well-being of civilians, and contributes to a more just and peaceful global community.

The concept of *Innere Führung*, developed in West Germany after World War II, has given rise to the notion of soldiers as citizens in uniform and emphasized their role in upholding democratic principles and human rights. It has helped to transform soldiers from mere instruments of state power into virtuous and moral actors who, even in the performance of their military duties, are encouraged to go beyond "unconditional obedience" and instead actively consider their orders and actions; the individual conscience remains the final arbiter of what is right. This new ethic creates a close link between military service and the principles of democracy and motivates soldiers to show civil courage, stand up for justice, and consistently align their military duties with the democratic principles of the society that they protect. The soldier's mission is fulfilled in actively standing up for human dignity, freedom, peace, justice, equality, solidarity, and democracy as the values that undergird the state.

However, this new ethical orientation must not abstract from the brutal hardships of military operations – both experienced and feared. The physical wounds suffered in combat often force military personnel to undergo a long and arduous process of physical and emotional rehabilitation, often accompanied by a deep sense of loss. Equally debilitating are the psychological and moral wounds suffered during deployment. Psychological and moral wounds significantly impair soldiers' ability to reintegrate into their predeployment lives. Exposure to extreme suffering, violence, and death during deployment changes their view of the world around them and makes everyday life and the concerns of their home country seem trivial. This dissonance can trigger a sense of marginalization or alienation as veterans struggle to reconcile their experiences with civilian life. As a result, many veterans suffer from mental health issues such as posttraumatic stress disorder (PTSD), anxiety, and depression, underscoring the lasting effects of their service.

Here, then, are a few of the main findings of our project of character formation and ethical education in late modern pluralistic societies. This short book, and the ten volumes it distills, is offered as the start to a new conversation, not the final word. We have focused selectively on liberal societies in Germany, the United Kingdom, the United States, Australia, and South Africa, knowing that studies of other modern pluralistic societies will refine and revise, if not challenge and transform as needed, the preliminary picture that we have sketched here. We have focused primarily on historical and contemporary Catholic and Protestant scholars and scholarship, hoping that the insights of many other world religions and philosophies will deepen what we have offered so far. We have selected ten major modern social systems for analysis, while recognizing that there are other social systems, or other social divisions, that require analysis, especially as we widen the geopolitical range of this interdisciplinary study. Even with these limits, however, we hope that our project has succeeded in challenging the conventional understanding of pluralism as mere plurality, and encouraging readers to see that modern liberal societies comprise a variety of social systems or social spheres, which interact with each other and with individuals in complex ways. While any of these spheres or their combinations can become dangerous and damaging, they are nonetheless essential for the preservation and flourishing of complex liberal societies, and they play critical roles in the character formation and ethical education of each new generation of individual members.

www.ingramcontent.com/pod-product-compliance
Lightning Source LLC
Chambersburg PA
CBHW072154160426
43197CB00012B/2376